NOT LEFT BEHIND

A Tribulation Survival Guide

Copyright © 2015 Glenn Tuley
Create Space Version
ISBN: 978-1518842597
Published in the United States of America

All rights reserved as permitted under the U. S. Copyright Act of 1976. No part of this publication may be reproduced, distributed, or transmitted in any form or by any means, or stored in a database or retrieval system, without the expressed written permission of the author and publisher.

Unless otherwise identified, all Scripture quotations have been taken from THE HOLY BIBLE, NEW INTERNATIONAL VERSION®, NIV® Copyright © 1973, 1978, 1984, 2011 by Biblica, Inc.® Used by permission. All rights reserved worldwide.

BurkhartBooks
www.burkhartbooks.com
Bedford, Texas

Dedication

This work is dedicated to King Jesus, whose Word says:

> *Keep your lives free from the love of money*
> *and be content with what you have,*
> *because God has said,*
>
> *"Never will I leave you;*
> *never will I forsake you."*
> *So we say with confidence,*
>
> *"The Lord is my helper; I will not be afraid.*
> *What can mere mortals do to me?"*

Hebrews 13:5 & 6

Acknowledgments

I would like to thank Larry Booth, who encouraged me to type up the notes what were the basis of this book.

I would like to thank Tim P. Taylor, who got me seriously thinking about publishing this book.

But most of all, I would like to thank my wife, Barbara, who has loved and supported me these last 40 years!

Contents

Dedication
Acknowledgments
Preface
Introduction — xi
Chapter 1 - The Beginning of the End — 13
Chapter 2 - Really Tough Times — 23
Chapter 3 - Events in Mark not mentioned in Matthew — 33
Chapter 4 - Events in Luke not mentioned in Matthew or Mark — 39
Chapter 5 - First Corinthians — 45
Chapter 6 - Philippians — 47
Chapter 7 - First Thessalonians — 49
Chapter 8 - Second Thessalonians — 55
Chapter 9 - Second Peter — 59
Chapter 10 - Jeremiah — 67
Chapter 11 - Isaiah — 71
Chapter 12 - Ezekiel — 77
Chapter 13 - Daniel — 93
Chapter 14 - Joel — 107
Chapter 15 - Zechariah — 113
Chapter 16 - Malachi — 121
Chapter 17 - Amos — 125
Chapter 18 - Zephaniah — 127
Chapter 19 - Revelation — 131
Chapter 20 - How Should We Live? — 141
About the Author

Preface

In 2005 I had a dream that I was in a meeting with a group of church leaders. During a break in the meeting the attendees clustered in smaller groups and discussed the previous speakers address. I wasn't in a discussion, but overheard a comment by a man, who in the dream, everyone understood to be a prophet. He said "Today is the first day of the second year of the Tribulation."

My first thought was, "This must be a dream."

In my dream, I tried to get closer to the prophet to ask some questions. My big question was "Is the 'today' in this dream today or some future day?" I woke up before I could ask the question.

My question sent me to the Scriptures to determine the answer to my question. I quickly came to the conclusion that the "today" in my dream was some future day. Then I started writing down all the Scriptures that I could find that describe the Tribulation, because I thought it would be useful for the church to know the characteristics of the Tribulation.

My notes stayed in the back of my Bible for about a year until my pastor said something in a sermon that prompted me to show him my notes the following week. He encouraged me to type up my notes and to give him a copy. This book is an extension of my typing those notes.

Introduction

I grew up in churches that taught that the Rapture (Jesus returning for Christians and taking them away to Heaven) takes place right before the Tribulation starts. In the summer of 1971, I read the first edition of Hal Lindsey's *The Late Great Planet Earth* and at that time thought it correctly interpreted the events of the End Times.

Over the next 20 years and through reading the Bible through several times in the *King James Version*, *New American Standard Version*, and *New International Version*, I have come to the conclusion that you can only arrive at the Pre-Tribulation Rapture position, by ignoring key verses of Scripture and ignoring the context of other verses.

My purpose in writing this book is not to debate the Pre-, Mid-, and Post-Rapture positions or even the Preterist interpretation. When Jesus returns, He is not going to make adjustments to fit our eschatological positions.

My purpose is to list all descriptions of the Tribulation in Scripture, so that we will be able to know if we are in the Tribulation period.

In this book, I will not quote authorities or experts. I may say "Some people say..." for the purpose of comparing a teaching to Scripture, but Scripture is the only real authority. Any teaching that contradicts Scripture is heresy. The

Holy Spirit inspired Scripture and He will not contradict Himself by giving another teaching to anyone.

We must be very careful how we interpret what we believe the Lord is telling us about the future. We humans have a tendency to interpret things the way we want them to be. Remember, the Lord's interpretation is the only one that really matters.

In the first edition of *The Late Great Planet Earth*, Hal Lindsey included his speculation that Jesus would return in 1988. I hope to avoid making the same type of error. Unlike Hal Lindsey, I read Matthew 24:3-31 as a timeline given by Jesus and the paragraphs that follow in chapter 24 and 25 are teachings and parables that relate to understanding the timeline and are not part of the timeline.

My ultimate purpose in writing this book is to get the readers prepared to meet their Maker. In the church where I was a member for twenty two years, there were a pair signs (by each of the main exits) that said, "We exist to glorify God and to make Him known!" I hope this book contributes to that ultimate purpose.

Chapter 1

THE BEGINNING OF THE END

Jesus answered: "Watch out that no one deceives you. For many will come in my name, claiming, 'I am the Christ,' and will deceive many."
(Matthew 24:4-5)

Matthew was written around 50 AD.

Glenn Tuley

Jesus answered: "Watch out that no one deceives you. For many will come in my name, claiming, 'I am the Christ,' and will deceive many."
(Matthew 24:4-5)

Whenever I read this passage, I wonder who are the people that get deceived and how are they deceived.

Jesus said to them: "Watch out that no one deceives you. Many will come in my name, claiming, 'I am he,' and will deceive many."
(Mark 13:5-6)

Obviously, they will be people who do not get the warning (or discount it). Those that will be deceived probably are not people who know their Bible. The Church (all denominations) needs to take the part of the Great Commission about "making disciples" (Matthew 28:19) more seriously.

Because Jesus said that many would be deceived, we know that there is a limit to our ability to prevent people from being deceived, however, that doesn't mean that we shouldn't make sure that as few as possible of the deceived come from the Church.

You will hear of wars and rumors of wars, but

Not Left Behind

see to it that you are not alarmed. Such things must happen, but the end is still to come.
(Matthew 24:6)

Since the end of World War II, we have seen wars and rumors of wars. Every year since then from 1946-2007, at least one war or civil war has started. There has not been a single year without multiple ongoing wars.

When you hear of wars and rumors of wars, do not be alarmed. Such things must happen, but the end is still to come.
(Mark 13:7)

There have been over 180 wars since World War II, including 56 wars and civil wars that are on-going while I write this paragraph (for a current list of on-going conflicts, see http://en.wikipedia.org/wiki/Ongoing_conflicts).

Note that Jesus tells us not to be alarmed. Just as on the Sea of Galilee, when the winds and waves obeyed him, he is still in control.

Nation will rise against nation, and kingdom against kingdom. There will be famines and earthquakes in various places. All these are the beginning of birth pains.
(Matthew 24:7-8)

Glenn Tuley

In Matthew, Mark, and Luke, Jesus tells us that there will be multiple wars fought by multiple countries. Some think this refers to World War I and World War II. That could be correct or it could be a reference to events like Operation Desert Storm and Operation Iraqi Freedom, where coalitions of nations joined together and there was a lot of talk of war for a long time before the shooting started.

> *Nation will rise against nation, and kingdom against kingdom. There will be earthquakes in various places, and famines. These are the beginning of birth pains.*
>
> (Mark 13:8)

Famines can be caused by weather or they can be caused by tyrants trying to control people or a side effect of warfare as we have seen in Somalia, the Sudan, Zimbabwe, North Korea, and other places.

> *Then he said to them: "Nation will rise against nation, and kingdom against kingdom. There will be great earthquakes, famines and pestilences in various places, and fearful events and great signs from heaven."*
>
> (Luke 21:10-11)

Not Left Behind

Note that in Luke, Jesus adds pestilences, which are fatal epidemic diseases. Do AIDS and the avian bird flu qualify?

If all that is not bad enough, Jesus tells us in Matthew and Mark that these are only "the beginning of birth pains." When a woman is having a baby, the discomfort of the baby coming out starts slowly and then increases in severity and frequency. I believe Jesus is telling us that things are going to be very difficult before the blessed event of his Second Coming, but like the pains of childbirth, it will be worth it.

> *Then you will be handed over to be persecuted and put to death, and you will be hated by all nations because of me.*
> (Matthew 24:9)

While we do not yet experience this in North America, this does happen in other countries.

> *You must be on your guard. You will be handed over to the local councils and flogged in the synagogues. On account of me you will stand before governors and kings as witnesses to them.*
> (Mark 13:9)

Persecution will come from religious leaders and will result in witnessing to the highest leaders in government. This happened with the Apostle Paul in the book of Acts, so it should not be a surprise to us if it happens again during the Tribulation.

> *At that time many will turn away from the faith and will betray and hate each other, and many false prophets will appear and deceive many people.*
>
> (Matthew 24:10-11)

This is, for me, one of the most troubling passages in Scripture. I can understand how false prophets will appear and lead many people astray, but people turning away from the faith is the hard part to comprehend. I grew up in a church that preached "once saved, always saved," so turning away from the faith, "does not compute" easily.

Over the years, I have given a lot of thought to this issue. In Egypt, you get a national ID card with "Christian" in the Religion field, if your father is labeled "Christian" on his national ID card. In North America we don't have national ID card with a space for religion, but our culture often considers someone a "Christian," if they do not proclaim Atheism or some other religion. I refer to these people as "Cultural Christians," as differentiated from people who are Christians based upon a personal relationship with Jesus Christ.

Not Left Behind

Cultural Christians who are exposed to the faith could more easily reject and turn away from the faith, than those with a personal relationship with Jesus. Even in North America, we have already seen Cultural Christians refer to Bible believing Christians as "narrow minded" or other less complimentary terms.

There is, however, one group of Christians that I could see very easily getting disillusioned during the Tribulation and turning away from the faith. Some who hold to the belief that Jesus' return will mark the beginning of the Tribulation rather than the end of it, may reject everything about Christianity, rather than choosing to reexamine Scripture and their interpretations.

How could false prophets deceive many people? The best inoculation I know against getting deceived is knowing the truth. Churches need to encourage more Bible reading. I am hesitant to recommend memorization, mainly because I was never that good at it. But we need to at least read the Bible enough so that we can recognize when someone is twisting the meaning by slightly misquoting Scripture.

People who are trained to look for counterfeit money, train by examining real money, then they will know when something is not quite right. Likewise, we should know the Scriptures well enough to know when a teaching is "not quite right!"

Glenn Tuley

Because of the increase of wickedness, the love of most will grow cold, but he who stands firm to the end will be saved.

(Matthew 24:12-13)

This sentence is one used by advocates of Pre-Tribulation Rapture to argue that the increase of wickedness is the result of the Christians being raptured and the Holy Spirit leaving the Earth with them. In the Twentieth Century there had been an increase in wickedness (Stalin, Hitler, the Holocaust, Bosnia, Somalia, Southern Sudan, Darfur, just to name a few) that were pretty awful without having the Church raptured.

And the gospel must first be preached to all nations.

(Mark 13:10)

And this gospel of the kingdom will be preached in the whole world as a testimony to all nations, and then the end will come.

(Matthew 24:14)

Earlier (in Matthew 24:8), Jesus refers to events as being only the beginning of birth pains. Here he declares that the end will come when this gospel of the kingdom will be preached in the whole world as a testimony to all nations.

The Gospel has been preached in every country, but "to all nations" implies that all

Not Left Behind

the people of those nations would be able to understand it. Several missions organizations are working to be able to present the Gospel in the native languages of the people who have not yet heard the good news of Jesus.

Note that Mark 13:10 is sandwiched between two verses that talk about persecution of Christians and verse 11 says, "Whenever you are arrested and brought to trial, do not worry beforehand about what to say. Just say whatever is given you at the time, for it is not you speaking, but the Holy Spirit."

Before we move on, let's stop and take a look at the big picture and see what we know so far.

1. There will be deceivers who will deceive many.

2. There will be wars and rumors of war.

3. There will be famines and earthquakes and pestilences in various places.

4. There will be persecution of followers of Jesus: some will be killed, but they will be hated in all nations.

5. Many will turn away from the faith, betraying and hating each other.

6. Many false prophets will appear.

7. The gospel of the kingdom will be preached in the whole world.

Most of the above have occurred or are in the process of happening. For some of the items it is only a matter of degree before they are fulfilled.

Chapter 2

REALLY TOUGH TIMES

So when you see standing in the holy place "the abomination that causes desolation," spoken of through the prophet Daniel—let the reader understand—then let those who are in Judea flee to the mountains. Let no one on the roof of his house go down to take anything out of the house. Let no one in the field go back to get his cloak. How dreadful it will be in those days for pregnant women and nursing mothers! Pray that your flight will not take place in winter or on the Sabbath.

(MATTHEW 24:15-20)

Glenn Tuley

To understand this passage, we need to look at what Daniel recorded centuries earlier.

> *He will confirm a covenant with many for one "seven." In the middle of the "seven" he will put an end to sacrifice and offering. And on a wing of the temple he will set up an abomination that causes desolation, until the end that is decreed is poured out on him.*
>
> (Daniel 9:27)

Daniel was visited by the Angel Gabriel, who explained a vision to him, that had its immediate fulfillment by Antiochus Epiphanies IV in 168 BC, when he transformed the Temple, rebuilt after the Babylonian Captivity, into a pagan temple.

> *His armed forces will rise up to desecrate the temple fortress and will abolish the daily sacrifice. Then they will set up the abomination that causes desolation.*
>
> (Daniel 11:31)

Jesus' reference to the prophesy in Daniel means that something similar will happen again.

Daniel's prophesy of *"70 weeks"* (commonly interpreted as 70 sets of 7's or 70 times 7 years) has a missing period of 7 that commonly referred

Not Left Behind

to as the 7 years of the Tribulation.

From the time that the daily sacrifice is abolished and the abomination that causes desolation is set up, there will be 1,290 days.

(Daniel 12:11)

Daniel refers to daily sacrifice being abolished, as it was by Antiochus Epiphanies IV, but Jesus does not specifically mention it. Therefore, I do not believe that rebuilding the Temple is a necessary requirement for Jesus to return, but it is clear that something will occur half-way through the Tribulation on the Temple Mount that will be clearly offensive to Jewish worship.

It will be a time to "head for the hills!" Why flee to the mountains? Because militarily, mountains provide more easily defensible positions than open fields or cities. Mountains also provide some protection against nuclear and other weapons.

Some teachers say that since there was about 1,290 years from the ending of the daily sacrifice at the fall of Jerusalem to the Babylonians until the building of the Dome on the Rock, that must be what Daniel is talking about. The problem with this interpretation is the building of the Dome on the Rock was not a signal to flee, since the Arab armies had recently captured Jerusalem. If anyone was going to flee they should have done so already.

Glenn Tuley

For false Christs and false prophets will appear and perform great signs and miracles to deceive even the elect—if that were possible.

(Matthew 24:24)

Some of these false Christs and false prophets will perform some pretty amazing signs and miracles. The signs and miracles will have to be amazing to deceive large numbers of people.

One more reason for the Church to make sure their members know Scripture. It is only by knowing the Scriptures well that one can tell that someone claiming to speak for God is subtly perverting Scripture.

At that time if anyone says to you, "Look, here is the Christ!" or, "Look, there he is!" do not believe it. For false Christs and false prophets will appear and perform signs and miracles to deceive the elect—if that were possible. So be on your guard; I have told you everything ahead of time.

(Mark 13:21-22)

In Acts 17:11, Luke commends the attenders of the synagogue in Berea because they "examined the Scriptures every day to see if what Paul said was true." This is the best insurance against false teachers!

Jesus clearly tells us to not follow reports of

Not Left Behind

Him returning in obscure or remote places.

So if anyone tells you, "There he is, out in the desert," do not go out; or, "Here he is, in the inner rooms," do not believe it. For as lightning that comes from the east is visible even in the west, so will be the coming of the Son of Man.
(Matthew 24:26-27)

Using the analogy of lightning, Jesus tells us that His return will be visible by everyone. Whether He was telling us that his return will be literally visible or visible everywhere because of the technological advances of the last 50 years really does not matter. We will know it when we see it!

Immediately after the distress of those days the sun will be darkened, and the moon will not give its light; the stars will fall from the sky, and the heavenly bodies will be shaken.
(Matthew 24:29)

The stars of heaven and their constellations will not show their light. The rising sun will be darkened and the moon will not give its light.
(Isaiah 13:10)

This is a quote from the prophet Isaiah, telling

Glenn Tuley

what the Lord showed him about the destruction of Babylon. The specific quote is from Isaiah 13:10, where he is describing the time just before verse 11 that says "I will punish the world for its evil, the wicked for their sins." Right before Jesus returns there will be signs in the sun, moon and sky that will get the world's attention.

> *At that time the sign of the Son of Man will appear in the sky, and all the nations of the earth will mourn. They will see the Son of Man coming on the clouds of the sky, with power and great glory. And he will send his angels with a loud trumpet call, and they will gather his elect from the four winds, from one end of the heavens to the other.*
> (Matthew 24: 30-31)

> *But in those days, following that distress, the sun will be darkened, and the moon will not give its light; the stars will fall from the sky, and the heavenly bodies will be shaken.*

> *At that time men will see the Son of Man coming in clouds with great power and glory. And he will send his angels and gather his elect from the four winds, from the ends of the earth to the ends of the heavens.*
> (Mark 13:24-27)

Not Left Behind

Jesus tells us that He will return appearing in the sky right after the sun and moon are darkened. Since He is called "the Light of the World" there is no doubt that it will be a dramatic appearance!

If you do research into appearances of Jesus in people's dreams there is one common striking feature of these dreams. Everyone, Christians and non-Christians, knows that it is Jesus. He needs no introduction! When Jesus returns, "all the nations of the earth will mourn," because even those who have rejected Him will know that He is returning for judgment.

> *At that time they will see the Son of Man coming in a cloud with power and great glory.*
> (Luke 21:27)

Jesus will send his angels off in every directions to gather his elect. Note that the gathering of the elect (the Rapture) takes place after everything that we have described previously (the abomination that causes desolation, false prophets, stars falling from the skies, etc.). This definitely indicates a post-Tribulation Rapture.

> *Now learn this lesson from the fig tree: As soon as its twigs get tender and its leaves come out, you know that summer is near. Even so, when you see all these things, you know that it is near, right at*

Glenn Tuley

the door. I tell you the truth, this generation will certainly not pass away until all these things have happened. Heaven and earth will pass away, but my words will never pass away.

(Matthew 24:32-35)

Many have interpreted the parable of the fig tree to mean that the generation that sees the rebirth of the nation of Israel will also see the return of Jesus. The major problem I see with this interpretation is that Israel is usually portrayed as an olive tree rather than a fig tree, although He had recently cursed a fig tree for not having fruit even though it had leaves, implying that it had fruit.

A general interpretation of Matthew 24:32-35, that is fully consistent with Scripture, tells us to be aware of the seasons and that the generation that sees everything come together will not pass away until Jesus returns.

> *As it was in the days of Noah, so it will be at the coming of the Son of Man. For in the days before the flood, people were eating and drinking, marrying and giving in marriage, up to the day Noah entered the ark; and they knew nothing about what would happen until the flood came and took them all away. That is how it will be at the coming of the Son of Man.*
>
> (Matthew 24:37-39)

Not Left Behind

With all that Jesus describes before Matthew 24:37, the only people who could be clueless about what is happening are those who choose to be clueless. Note that starting in Verse 37, Jesus is making a comparison to the days of Noah as a means of further explaining what he has described before.

> *Just as it was in the days of Noah, so also will it be in the days of the Son of Man. People were eating, drinking, marrying and being given in marriage up to the day Noah entered the ark. Then the flood came and destroyed them all.*
> (Luke 17:26-27)

No doubt, there were many people who asked Noah and his sons what they were building, since it took about 100 years to build (Genesis 6 and 7). The only way they could be caught by surprise it to chose to not believe and continue their way of life.

Why do people reject Jesus today? It is not because of the historical facts, but rather the fact that they do not want to submit to Jesus and His demands for Lordship. Just as in the days of Noah, people do not want to change the way they live their lives.

> *Therefore keep watch, because you do not know on what day your Lord will come. But understand this: If the owner of the house had known at what time of night the thief was coming, he would have kept watch and would not have let his house be broken into. So you also must be ready, because the Son of Man will come at an hour when you do not expect him.*
>
> (Matthew 24:42-44)

Jesus is telling us that we don't know exactly when He will return, but we are to be ready for His return. The Parable of the 10 Virgins and the Parable of the Talents in the next chapter (Matthew 25) reinforce the necessity to be prepared.

Chapter 3

Events in Mark not mentioned in Matthew

Mark was written in the 50s or 60s AD.

In the first two chapters, we looked at the events leading up to Jesus' return based on the sequence of events in Matthew along with verses from other books that directly correlate. In this chapter we will look at passages from Mark the describe End Times happenings that are not specifically mentioned in Matthew.

Glenn Tuley

Brother will betray brother to death, and a father his child. Children will rebel against their parents and have them put to death.

(Mark 13:12)

We haven't seen family betrayals in North America, yet, but it has not been uncommon in places like the former Soviet Union, China, and Muslim countries.

You will be betrayed even by parents, brothers, relatives and friends, and they will put some of you to death.

(Luke 21:16)

All men will hate you because of me, but he who stands firm to the end will be saved.

(Mark 13:13)

All men will hate you because of me.

(Luke 21:17)

In communist countries being a Christian was tolerated as long as you kept your religion to yourself and did not "proselytize." In most communist countries, providing religious instruction to children was a crime. In Saudi Arabia, and some other Muslim countries, it is a crime punishable by death to convert from Islam

Not Left Behind

and to become a Christian.

Christians will become unpopular in society because of Jesus. Christians are often portrayed as "unloving" if they oppose "a woman's right to choose" to kill her own offspring. In Canada, pastors risk arrest for "hate crimes" if they mention Scriptures that condemn homosexuality.

Jesus calls us to be faithful, even, or I should say, especially when it is unpopular. Luke 21:18 reminds me of Daniel 3:26-27:

> *Nebuchadnezzar then approached the opening of the blazing furnace and shouted, "Shadrach, Meshach and Abednego, servants of the Most High God, come out! Come here!"*
>
> *So Shadrach, Meshach and Abednego came out of the fire, and the satraps, prefects, governors and royal advisers crowded around them. They saw that the fire had not harmed their bodies, nor was a hair of their heads singed; their robes were not scorched, and there was no smell of fire on them.*

Shadrach, Meshach, and Abednego were faithful and the Lord protected them from the fiery furnace. But just as significant as the miraculous protection, was their determination to remain faithful to the Lord before they were thrown into the fiery furnace (Daniel 3:17-18):

Glenn Tuley

If we are thrown into the blazing furnace, the God we serve is able to save us from it, and he will rescue us from your hand, O king. But even if he does not, we want you to know, O king, that we will not serve your gods or worship the image of gold you have set up.

Whether God chooses to be glorified by our martyrdom or to keep us safe is God's choice not ours. He calls us to be faithful.

If anyone is ashamed of me and my words in this adulterous and sinful generation, the Son of Man will be ashamed of him when he comes in his Father's glory with the holy angels.

(Mark 8:38)

When we are led to the lions in the Coliseum like the early Christians, we need to be faithful, as though our souls depended on it.

How dreadful it will be in those days for pregnant women and nursing mothers! Pray that this will not take place in winter, because those will be days of distress unequaled from the beginning, when God created the world, until now—and never to be equaled again.

(Mark 13:17-19)

"Those days" are the time of "the abomination that causes desolation" when those in Judea are

Not Left Behind

to flee to the mountains. Note that Jesus tells us to pray that it doesn't take place in the winter, when travel would be more difficult.

How dreadful it will be in those days for pregnant women and nursing mothers! There will be great distress in the land and wrath against this people.
(Luke 21:23)

Those will be days of distress unequaled from the beginning, when God created the world, until now—and never to be equaled again. That means worse than anything we have ever seen. Worse than the Holocaust. Worse than everything!

If the Lord had not cut short those days, no one would survive.
(Mark 13:20)

Yes, they will be dreadful days, but the Lord cuts them short, because He is in control!

Chapter 4

Events in Luke not mentioned in Matthew or Mark

Luke was written before 63 AD.

Glenn Tuley

Answering the Pharisees Questions

> *Once, having been asked by the Pharisees when the kingdom of God would come, Jesus replied, "The kingdom of God does not come with your careful observation, nor will people say, 'Here it is,' or 'There it is,' because the kingdom of God is within you."*
>
> (Luke 17:20-21)

The Pharisees were probably wondering when He was going to establish His kingdom and throw the Romans out, as Barabbas attempted. Jesus answered that the kingdom of God is within us. Of course, it is only within us when we make Jesus the King of our lives.

> *Then he said to his disciples, "The time is coming when you will long to see one of the days of the Son of Man, but you will not see it. Men will tell you, 'There he is!' or 'Here he is!' Do not go running off after them. For the Son of Man in his day will be like the lightning, which flashes and lights up the sky from one end to the other. But first he must suffer many things and be rejected by this generation."*
>
> (Luke 17:22-25)

Jesus then tells his disciples that they will miss

Not Left Behind

him when He leaves them and that they should not chase after reports of his appearing here and there (and neither should we). When Jesus returns, He will want everyone to know it: *"For the Son of Man in his day will be like the lightning, which flashes and lights up the sky from one end to the other."*

> *With one voice they cried out, "Away with this man! Release Barabbas to us!"*
> (Luke 23:18)
>
> *But they kept shouting, "Crucify him! Crucify him!"*
> (Luke 23:21)

However, He knows that some of his listeners believe He is going to set up His Kingdom soon, so He continues: *"But first he must suffer many things and be rejected by this generation."*

Answering the Disciples questions

> *But before all this, they will lay hands on you and persecute you. They will deliver you to synagogues and prisons, and you will be brought before kings and governors, and all on account of my name. This will result in your being witnesses to them.*
> (Luke 21:12-13)

Glenn Tuley

While *"But before all this"* could refer to a time directly before the Tribulation, this has been happening since the First Century. While it has been a long time since Christians have been turned over to a synagogue, they are thrown into prison and brought before government officials all the time in many countries of the world. Even in the United States and Canada, Christians have been fined and threatened with jail time for refusing to celebrate lifestyles that are contrary to the clear teachings of Scripture, in spite of religious freedom guarantees.

> *When you see Jerusalem surrounded by armies, you will know that its desolation is near. Then let those who are in Judea flea to the mountains. Let those who are in the city go out and those in the country not enter the city. For this is the time of punishment in fulfillment of all that has been written. How dreadful it will be in those days for pregnant women and nursing mothers! There will be great distress in the land and wrath against this people. They will fall by the sword and will be taken as prisoners to all the nations. Jerusalem will be trampled on by the Gentiles until the times of the Gentiles are fulfilled.*
>
> (Luke 21:20-24)

This is one of the passages that could be talking

about the destruction of Jerusalem in 70 AD or the End Times or both.

If this passage was not in the context of Jesus describing the end times, one could say that it is clearly describing 70 AD. Yes, it fits 70 AD, but since the larger context of the passage is the End Times, one has to say this passage applies to both.

The last sentence is most interesting: "Jerusalem will be trampled on by the Gentiles until the times of the Gentiles are fulfilled." The Jewish nation was not in control of the old city of Jerusalem from 70 AD until the "6 Day War" in June 1967. Many have argued that this marks the last generation that will see the return of the Messiah. As I write this in October 2007, I do not see a lot of the other signs I would expect to see if this (1967+40=2007) were a correct interpretation.

An alternative interpretation is that the generation that saw the end of the trampling of Jerusalem by Gentiles would see the events of the Tribulation and Jesus' Return. Someone like me who was 13 (one Jewish definition of adulthood) in June 1967, could reasonably expect to live until about 2030. So, if this interpretation is correct, we would expect to see the events of the Tribulation starting no later than 2023.

Glenn Tuley

There will be signs in the sun, moon and stars. On the earth, nations will be in anguish and perplexity at the roaring and tossing of the sea.
(Luke 21:25)

Matthew 24:29 describes signs in the "sun, moon and stars," but does not mention "the roaring and tossing of the sea." Any number of things can cause "roaring and tossing of the sea," earthquakes or asteroids or meteors hitting the oceans or even California sliding into the ocean.

Men will faint from terror, apprehensive of what is coming on the world, for the heavenly bodies will be shaken.
(Luke 21:26)

This is between the "signs in the sun, moon and stars" and "at that time they will see the Son of Man coming in a cloud with power and great glory." From the context we know that the men who "will faint from terror" are not Christians who know their Bibles. How can I say this? Verse 28 says, *"When these things begin to take place, stand up and lift up your heads, because your redemption is drawing near."* Those who know their Bibles will know that Jesus is coming soon!

Chapter 5

FIRST CORINTHIANS

Written about 55 AD.

Glenn Tuley

Then the end will come, when he hands over the kingdom to God the Father after he has destroyed all dominion, authority and power. For he must reign until he has put all his enemies under his feet. The last enemy to be destroyed is death.

(1 Corinthians 15:24-26)

Paul is writing to the church in Corinth refuting claims by some that there is no resurrection of the dead. The "he" in this passage is Jesus. When Jesus returns, He will take control and destroy "all dominion, authority and power." Jesus will be in charge.

Listen, I tell you a mystery: We will not all sleep, but we will all be changed— in a flash, in the twinkling of an eye, at the last trumpet. For the trumpet will sound, the dead will be raised imperishable, and we will be changed. For the perishable must clothe itself with the imperishable, and the mortal with immortality.

(1 Corinthians 15:51-53)

In this passage Paul uses "sleep" as a euphemism for "death." We will not all die. Those of us who are still alive "at the last trumpet" will be given their imperishable eternal bodies at the same time as those resurrected from the dead.

Chapter 6

PHILIPPIANS

WRITTEN ABOUT 54 AD.

Glenn Tuley

And this is my prayer: that your love may abound more and more in knowledge and depth of insight, so that you may be able to discern what is best and may be pure and blameless until the day of Christ, filled with the fruit of righteousness that comes through Jesus Christ—to the glory and praise of God.
(Philippians 1:9-11)

Paul is praying for the church in Philippi that their love would abound, that they will have knowledge and depth of insight, that they would be able to discern what is best, that they would be pure and blameless until the day of Christ, and that they would be filled with the fruit of righteousness that comes through Christ.

Do everything without complaining or arguing, so that you may become blameless and pure, children of God without fault in a crooked and depraved generation, in which you shine like stars in the universe as you hold out the word of life—in order that I may boast on the day of Christ that I did not run or labor for nothing.
(Philippians 2:14-16)

Paul is telling the Philippians to live as children of God, blameless and pure lives, without fault, in a crooked and depraved generation. Paul did not want his work among them to be for nothing.

Chapter 7

First Thessalonians

Written about 54 AD.

Glenn Tuley

The Lord's message rang out from you not only in Macedonia and Achaia—your faith in God has become known everywhere. Therefore we do not need to say anything about it, for they themselves report what kind of reception you gave us. They tell how you turned to God from idols to serve the living and true God, and to wait for his Son from heaven, whom he raised from the dead—Jesus, who rescues us from the coming wrath.

(1 Thessalonians 1:8-10)

Paul is giving thanks for the faith of the church at Thessalonika and how they "serve the living and true God, and to wait for his Son from heaven, whom he raised from the dead—Jesus, who rescues us from the coming wrath."

Some have used this passage to say that the Rapture comes before the Tribulation. The only way you can do this is to assume that the "wrath" is the Tribulation and not the judgment after the Tribulation, in addition to ignoring the timeline in Matthew 24:3-31, which clearly places the gathering of the elect after the Tribulation.

Brothers, we do not want you to be ignorant about those who fall asleep, or to grieve like the rest of men, who have no hope. We believe that Jesus died and rose again and so we believe that God will bring with Jesus those who have fallen asleep

Not Left Behind

in him. According to the Lord's own word, we tell you that we who are still alive, who are left till the coming of the Lord, will certainly not precede those who have fallen asleep. For the Lord himself will come down from heaven, with a loud command, with the voice of the archangel and with the trumpet call of God, and the dead in Christ will rise first. After that, we who are still alive and are left will be caught up together with them in the clouds to meet the Lord in the air. And so we will be with the Lord forever. Therefore encourage each other with these words.

(1 Thessalonians 4:13-18)

Paul is writing to combat a teaching in Thessalonika that those who die before Jesus returns will have a sort of second class heavenly citizenship compared to those who are alive when Jesus returns.

Notice the sequence of events:

1. For the Lord himself will come down from heaven, with a loud command, with the voice of the archangel and with the trumpet call of God,

2. And the dead in Christ will rise first.

3. After that, we who are still alive and are left will

be caught up together with them in the clouds to meet the Lord in the air.

4. And so we will be with the Lord forever.

Those who die before Christ returns get raised first and those who are still alive will be caught up (raptured) to meet them in the air. Then we all will be with the Lord forever.
"Encourage one another with these words." Jesus and his followers win!

> *Now, brothers, about times and dates we do not need to write to you, for you know very well that the day of the Lord will come like a thief in the night. While people are saying, "Peace and safety," destruction will come on them suddenly, as labor pains on a pregnant woman, and they will not escape.*
>
> (1 Thessalonians 5:1-3)

While people are saying "Peace and safety," Jesus will come "like a thief in the night." Here is an interesting question: Who would be saying "Peace and Safety" just before Jesus returns? It doesn't seem to me that it would be people who know their Bible, especially since the above passage says that "destruction will come on them suddenly, as labor pains on a pregnant woman,

Not Left Behind

and they will not escape."

Most teachers who use this passage to argue that the Bible teaches that Jesus could return at any time, avoid the next verse.

> *But you, brothers, are not in darkness so that this day should surprise you like a thief.*
> (1 Thessalonians 5:4)

Jesus' return should not surprise believers who are not in darkness. Believers who know the Word of the Lord will not be surprised, when something predicted in the Bible happens.

> *You are all sons of the light and sons of the day. We do not belong to the night or to the darkness. So then, let us not be like others, who are asleep, but let us be alert and self-controlled. For those who sleep, sleep at night, and those who get drunk, get drunk at night. But since we belong to the day, let us be self-controlled, putting on faith and love as a breastplate, and the hope of salvation as a helmet. For God did not appoint us to suffer wrath but to receive salvation through our Lord Jesus Christ. He died for us so that, whether we are awake or asleep, we may live together with him. Therefore encourage one another and build each other up, just as in fact you are doing.*
> (1 Thessalonians 5:5-11)

Glenn Tuley

Paul encourages the believers in Thessalonika to keep alert and live self-controlled lives with faith and love and the hope of their salvation.

Chapter 8

Second Thessalonians

Written about 51 or 52 AD.

Glenn Tuley

Concerning the coming of our Lord Jesus Christ and our being gathered to him, we ask you, brothers, not to become easily unsettled or alarmed by some prophecy, report or letter supposed to have come from us, saying that the day of the Lord has already come. Don't let anyone deceive you in any way, for (that day will not come) until the rebellion occurs and the man of lawlessness is revealed, the man doomed to destruction. He will oppose and will exalt himself over everything that is called God or is worshiped, so that he sets himself up in God's temple, proclaiming himself to be God.

(2 Thessalonians 2:1-4)

Paul is warning the believers in the church at Thessalonika to *"not to become easily unsettled or alarmed by some prophecy, report or letter supposed to have come from us."* Someone had apparently circulated a false teaching, allegedly from Paul *"saying that the day of the Lord has already come."*

The day of the Lord will not come "until the rebellion occurs and the man of lawlessness is revealed, the man doomed to destruction." The *"man of lawlessness"* is the Antichrist. *"He will oppose and will exalt himself over everything that is called God or is worshiped, so that he sets himself up in God's temple, proclaiming himself to be God."* The Antichrist's proclamation that he is God is may be the abomination that causes desolation (Matthew 24:15, Daniel 9:27, Daniel 11:31, Daniel 12:11, and Mark 13:14).

> *Don't you remember that when I was with you I used to tell you these things? And now you know what is holding him back, so that he may be revealed at the proper time. For the secret power of lawlessness is already at work; but the one who now holds it back will continue to do so till he is taken out of the way.*
> (2 Thessalonians 2:5-7)

Paul is writing them that he is not telling them anything that he had not told them before when he was with them.

The man of lawlessness is being held back until the *"proper time."*

> *How dreadful it will be in those days for pregnant women and nursing mothers! There will be great distress in the land and wrath against this people.*
> (Luke 21:23)

Who is doing the restraining? The text is not clear. It could be the Holy Spirit or a particular unnamed angel. The important point for us is that the power of lawlessness is being restrained until the *"proper time."*

Glenn Tuley

And then the lawless one will be revealed, whom the Lord Jesus will overthrow with the breath of his mouth and destroy by the splendor of his coming. The coming of the lawless one will be in accordance with the work of Satan displayed in all kinds of counterfeit miracles, signs and wonders, and in every sort of evil that deceives those who are perishing. They perish because they refused to love the truth and so be saved.
(2 Thessalonians 2:8-10)

The "lawless one will be revealed" and "the Lord Jesus will overthrow him with the breath of his mouth and destroy" him "by the splendor of his coming."

The lawless one will be doing the work of Satan (the Deceiver). He will perform "all kinds of counterfeit miracles, signs and wonders," and "every sort of evil" to "deceive those who are perishing."

Those who perish, will perish "because they refused to love the truth and so be saved." Remember back in Matthew 24:14 that the Gospel will be preached to the whole world before end comes. This is right before the Antichrist makes himself known with the abomination that causes desolation.

Chapter 9

Second Peter

Written between 65 and 68 AD.

Glenn Tuley

And we have the word of the prophets made more certain, and you will do well to pay attention to it, as to a light shining in a dark place, until the day dawns and the morning star rises in your hearts. Above all, you must understand that no prophecy of Scripture came about by the prophet's own interpretation. For prophecy never had its origin in the will of man, but men spoke from God as they were carried along by the Holy Spirit.
(2 Peter 1:19-21)

In previous verses, Peter was writing about the first coming of Jesus and how it was the fulfillment of prophesies. Prophecies that have been fulfilled make it more certain that the future prophesies will come to pass. So, no matter how dark the times seem to be, "pay attention" to prophesies "as to a light shining in a dark place, until the day dawns and the morning star rises in your hearts." Jesus will return and He wins in the end.

For if God did not spare angels when they sinned, but sent them to hell, putting them into gloomy dungeons to be held for judgment; if he did not spare the ancient world when he brought the flood on its ungodly people, but protected Noah, a preacher of righteousness, and seven others; if he condemned the cities of Sodom and Gomorrah by burning them to ashes, and made them an example

Not Left Behind

of what is going to happen to the ungodly; and if he rescued Lot, a righteous man, who was distressed by the filthy lives of lawless men (for that righteous man, living among them day after day, was tormented in his righteous soul by the lawless deeds he saw and heard)— if this is so, then the Lord knows how to rescue godly men from trials and to hold the unrighteous for the day of judgment, while continuing their punishment.

(2 Peter 2:4-9)

Does prophesy come from the prophet? No, it comes from the Holy Spirit, who speaks through men telling them what to say or write.

But there were also false prophets among the people, just as there will be false teachers among you. They will secretly introduce destructive heresies, even denying the sovereign Lord who bought them—bringing swift destruction on themselves. Many will follow their shameful ways and will bring the way of truth into disrepute. In their greed these teachers will exploit you with stories they have made up. Their condemnation has long been hanging over them, and their destruction has not been sleeping.

(2 Peter 2:1-3)

Peter warns that false teachers will deny the

sovereignty of the Lord. False teachers usually lie to themselves saying that commands of the Lord on how to live do not apply to themselves. As a result many who follow them adopt their lifestyle and "follow their shameful ways and will bring the way of truth into disrepute." The Gospel always suffers when those who claim to be Christians to do live like Christ.

Teaching that is not firmly rooted in Scripture is dangerous. What false teaching is Peter referring to? I don't think it matters. We should compare all teaching with Scripture. If a teaching and Scripture do not agree, then we know which is correct. Condemnation and destruction are awaiting false teachers.

> *For if God did not spare angels when they sinned, but sent them to hell, putting them in chains of darkness to be held for judgment; if he did not spare the ancient world when he brought the flood on its ungodly people, but protected Noah, a preacher of righteousness, and seven others; if he condemned the cities of Sodom and Gomorrah by burning them to ashes, and made them an example of what is going to happen to the ungodly; and if he rescued Lot, a righteous man, who was distressed by the depraved conduct of the lawless (for that righteous man, living among them day after day, was tormented in his righteous soul by the lawless*

Not Left Behind

deeds he saw and heard)—if this is so, then the Lord knows how to rescue the godly from trials and to hold the unrighteous for punishment on the day of judgment. This is especially true of those who follow the corrupt desire of the flesh and despise authority.

(2 Peter 2:4-10)

This passage is talking about protecting Noah and Lot from judgment, while their neighbors were destroyed by the judgment of God. Some use these verses as an argument that the Church will not go through the Tribulation, but the context does not justify such a conclusion. Just because God can protect us, does not mean that He will keep us from tough times by removing us from them. He can protect us in tough times without removing us from Earth.

But do not forget this one thing, dear friends: With the Lord a day is like a thousand years, and a thousand years are like a day. The Lord is not slow in keeping his promise, as some understand slowness. He is patient with you, not wanting anyone to perish, but everyone to come to repentance.

(2 Peter 3:8-9)

Verse 8 simply means that the Lord's timing is

not the same as ours.

God exists in eternity. We live in seconds, minutes, hours, days, months, years, and centuries. We only think about millennia (thousands of years).

The Lord will keep His promises. Just as He has been patient with each of us (not giving us what we deserve), He wants to give everyone the opportunity to repent. The Tribulation will be a last warning to repent.

But the day of the Lord will come like a thief. The heavens will disappear with a roar; the elements will be destroyed by fire, and the earth and everything in it will be laid bare.

> *Since everything will be destroyed in this way, what kind of people ought you to be? You ought to live holy and godly lives as you look forward to the day of God and speed its coming. That day will bring about the destruction of the heavens by fire, and the elements will melt in the heat. But in keeping with his promise we are looking forward to a new heaven and a new earth, the home of righteousness.*
>
> (2 Peter 3:10-13)

The "day of the Lord" is sometime (at least a few seconds) after the gathering of the elect. With heavens disappearing *"with a roar,"* and *"the*

Not Left Behind

elements" being *"destroyed by fire, and everything laid bare,"* it has to be after the gathering in order for their to be any people to gather.

> *How dreadful it will be in those days for pregnant women and nursing mothers! There will be great distress in the land and wrath against this people.*
> (Luke 21:23)

How should we live? *"You ought to live holy and godly lives as you look forward to the day of God and speed its coming."* We should live our lives in accordance with God's plans and priorities, not our own. Of course, the only way "to live holy and godly lives" is to make our thinking line up with God's thinking.

Chapter 10

JEREMIAH

Written between 626 and 586 BC.

Glenn Tuley

This is what the LORD, the God of Israel, says: "Write in a book all the words I have spoken to you. The days are coming," declares the LORD, "when I will bring my people Israel and Judah back from captivity and restore them to the land I gave their forefathers to possess," says the LORD.
(Jeremiah 30:2-3)

This has been happening since the end of World War II. The return to the land in the time of Ezra and Nehemiah was primarily a return of people from Judah, not "Israel and Judah."

These are the words the LORD spoke concerning Israel and Judah: This is what the LORD says:

"Cries of fear are heard—terror, not peace.

Ask and see:
Can a man bear children?
Then why do I see every strong man
with his hands on his stomach like a woman in labor, every face turned deathly pale?

How awful that day will be!
None will be like it.
It will be a time of trouble for Jacob,
but he will be saved out of it."
(Jeremiah 30:4-7)

Not Left Behind

The above could describe several times during the history of the people of Israel and Judah, however, note verse 7: "It will be a time of trouble for Jacob." The King James Version uses the phrase: "the time of Jacob's trouble." This is commonly interpreted to be the Tribulation Period. One could argue that this is describing the Holocaust, but the next passage shows it is yet to be completely fulfilled.

> *"In that day," declares the LORD Almighty," I will break the yoke off their necks and will tear off their bonds; no longer will foreigners enslave them. Instead, they will serve the LORD their God and David their king, whom I will raise up for them."*
> (Jeremiah 30:8-9)

The people of Israel and Judah may no longer be enslaved, but since the nation of Israel has yet to turn back to serving "the Lord their God" and the "son of David," we know this must be describing a future event.

Glenn Tuley

Chapter 11

ISAIAH

Written between 700 and 680 BC.

Glenn Tuley

Wail, for the day of the LORD is near; it will come like destruction from the Almighty. Because of this, all hands will go limp, every man's heart will melt. Terror will seize them, pain and anguish will grip them; they will writhe like a woman in labor. They will look aghast at each other, their faces aflame.
(Isaiah 13:6-8)

Isaiah is writing a prophesy against Babylon. It appears to have been largely fulfilled by the invasion of the Empire of the Medes and Persians that overthrew the Babylonian Empire. Because of the use of the term "the day of the Lord," many believe it also refers to the end times.

There will be signs in the sun, moon and stars. On the earth, nations will be in anguish and perplexity at the roaring and tossing of the sea. Men will faint from terror, apprehensive of what is coming on the world, for the heavenly bodies will be shaken.
(Luke 21:25-26)

When "the day of the Lord is near" Babylon is told to "wail," because "the day of the Lord is near" "will come like destruction from the Almighty." Isaiah says that "all hands will go limp" and "every man's heart will melt."

In verse 8 the phrase "Terror will seize them"

Not Left Behind

sounds similar to Luke 21:26, where Jesus says that "Men will faint from terror, apprehensive of what is coming on the world."

> *An oracle concerning Damascus: "See, Damascus will no longer be a city but will become a heap of ruins."*
>
> (Isaiah 17:1)

Damascus is one of the longest inhabited cities in the world. It has yet to become a heap of ruins. Currently it is the home of terrorist organizations like Hezbollah. Syria is ruled by the Baath Party (the same party also was in Iraq where it was lead by Saddam Hussein).

Unlike Jordan and Egypt, Syria did not signed a peace treaty with Israel after the Yom Kippur War in 1973 and is still in a technical state of war with Israel. Many believe that the reason no WMDs (weapons of mass destruction) were found during Operation Iraqi Freedom is that the WMDs were moved to Syria. On September 6, 2007 a reported nuclear facility was reportedly bombed in the Syria desert.

> *The cities of Aroer will be deserted and left to flocks, which will lie down, with no one to make them afraid.*
>
> (Isaiah 17:2)

Glenn Tuley

The cities of Aroer were at the southern end of the tribe of Reuben on the east side of the Jordan River. When Syria captured these lands it became Syria's southern border. The Jewish Encyclopedia says that ruins are located on the north bank of Arnon ravine about 11 miles from where it flows into the Dead Sea. (http://www.jewishencyclopedia.com/articles/1804-aroe)

> *"The fortified city will disappear from Ephraim, and royal power from Damascus; the remnant of Aram will be like the glory of the Israelites," declares the LORD Almighty.*
>
> (Isaiah 17:3)

Fortified cities disappeared from Ephraim (a synonym for the Kingdom of Israel) shortly after Isaiah wrote this. Royal power left Damascus when Syria was taken over by the Assyrian Empire.

The most interesting phrase is *"the remnant of Aram will be like the glory of the Israelites."* Aram was another name for the area around Damascus. Aramaic was the name of the language spoken by Jesus. This could be a prediction of the remnant of Aram turning to the Lord?

> *Do not be afraid, for I am with you;*
> *I will bring your children from the east*

Not Left Behind

and gather you from the west.
I will say to the north, "Give them up!"
and to the south, "Do not hold them back."
Bring my sons from afar
and my daughters from the ends of the earth—
everyone who is called by my name,
whom I created for my glory,
whom I formed and made.
Lead out those who have eyes but are blind,
who have ears but are deaf.

(Isaiah 43:5-8)

The people of Israel have been returning to Israel from every direction since the end of World War II.

All the nations gather together and the peoples assemble. Which of them foretold this and proclaimed to us the former things? Let them bring in their witnesses to prove they were right, so that others may hear and say, "It is true."

(Isaiah 43:9)

Where do all the nations gather and assemble? Representatives of all nations gathered together in May 1948 at the The United Nations General Assembly where they voted to partition the British Mandate into Israel and Trans-Jordan.

Chapter 12

EZEKIEL

Written between 593 and 573 BC.

Glenn Tuley

The word of the LORD came to me: "Son of man, set your face against Gog, of the land of Magog, the chief prince of Meshech and Tubal; prophesy against him and say: 'This is what the Sovereign LORD says: I am against you, O Gog, chief prince of Meshech and Tubal. I will turn you around, put hooks in your jaws and bring you out with your whole army—your horses, your horsemen fully armed, and a great horde with large and small shields, all of them brandishing their swords. Persia, Cush and Put will be with them, all with shields and helmets, also Gomer with all its troops, and Beth Togarmah from the far north with all its troops—the many nations with you.'"

(Ezekiel 38:1-6)

The first question that comes to my mind from this passage is: "Who are the people mentioned above?"

The sons of Japheth: Gomer, Magog, Madai, Javan, Tubal, Meshech and Tiras.

(Genesis 10:2)

The Book of Genesis tells us that Noah's son Japheth had seven sons and including the ones mentioned here: Magog, Meshech, Tubal, and Gomer. From Ezekiel, we can tell that Gog is

Not Left Behind

from Magog and the ruler of Meshech and Tubal. While writing this I did a search on Google for "Magog" and found a lot of theories about its location: from modern Turkey to Mongolia and just about everywhere in between. Tubal is the modern country of Georgia. Gomer has been associated with the area of modern Turkey where Paul wrote his letter to the Galatians, and also to the area of Armenia, and also to early residents of the Eurasian steppes where Germanic tribes lived. Beth Togarmah (or House of Togarmah) is Armenia. The sons of Japheth were the founders of the Caucasian race who lived to the north of Israel.

Persia officially changed its name to Iran in 1935. Cush was in the area of the Sudan and possibly northern Ethiopia. Put is the general area of Libya.

Coincidentally, this coalition is roughly the area of the Ottoman Empire at it's peak in the late 1600's plus Iran.

The Lord will draw out the armies of these many nations into a battle.

Get ready; be prepared, you and all the hordes gathered about you, and take command of them. After many days you will be called to arms. In future years you will invade a land that has recovered from war, whose people were gathered

Glenn Tuley

from many nations to the mountains of Israel, which had long been desolate. They had been brought out from the nations, and now all of them live in safety. You and all your troops and the many nations with you will go up, advancing like a storm; you will be like a cloud covering the land.
(Ezekiel 38:7-9)

The Lord tells these nations to *"Get ready; be prepared, you and all the hordes gathered about you,"* because they are going to *"be called to arms… after many days."* Some time in the distant future from the time Ezekiel wrote, they "will invade a land that has recovered from war, whose people were gathered from many nations to the mountains of Israel, which had long been desolate." When the Jewish people returned to the land after World War II, the land was desolate.

"They had been brought out from the nations, and now all of them live in safety." The Jewish people came back to Israel from a variety of nations. The prophesied attack will come when the Jewish people think they are living in safety. The advancing troops will move quickly like a storm front. They "will be like a cloud covering the land" which implies that they will overrun the land of Israel or at least a significant portion of it.

The first nine verses give an overview. The next passage gives some detail.

Not Left Behind

This is what the Sovereign LORD says: "On that day thoughts will come into your mind and you will devise an evil scheme. You will say, 'I will invade a land of unwalled villages; I will attack a peaceful and unsuspecting people—all of them living without walls and without gates and bars. I will plunder and loot and turn my hand against the resettled ruins and the people gathered from the nations, rich in livestock and goods, living at the center of the land.' Sheba and Dedan and the merchants of Tarshish and all her villages will say to you, 'Have you come to plunder? Have you gathered your hordes to loot, to carry off silver and gold, to take away livestock and goods and to seize much plunder?'"

(Ezekiel 38:10-13)

"The Sovereign LORD says" is a powerful statement. God is Sovereign! He is Lord! What He says shall come to pass! He says that these nations will have thoughts come to their minds, and "will devise and evil scheme" to "invade a land of unwalled villages" and "attack a peaceful and unsuspecting people" who live "without walls and without gates and bars" and to "plunder and loot" and hit "the people gathered from the nations, rich in livestock and goods living in the center of the land."

Glenn Tuley

The sons of Cush: Seba, Havilah, Sabtah, Raamah and Sabteca. The sons of Raamah: Sheba and Dedan.

(Genesis 10:7)

Abraham took another wife, whose name was Keturah. She bore him Zimran, Jokshan, Medan, Midian, Ishbak and Shuah. Jokshan was the father of Sheba and Dedan; the descendants of Dedan were the Asshurites, the Letushites and the Leummites.

(Genesis 25:1-3)

"Sheba and Dedan and the merchants of Tarshish and all her villages" will diplomatically question the coalition's intentions, but they do not appear to come to Israel's aid. One set of brothers named Sheba and Dedan were sons of Cush, grandson's of Ham, and great-grandsons of Noah. The other Sheba and Dedan were grandsons of Abraham through son, Jokshan born to his second wife Keturah after Sarah died.

Sheba (of Queen of Sheba fame) is generally thought to have existed near where the Red Sea opens into the Indian Ocean (Ethiopia on one side and modern Yemen on the other).

Isaiah 21:13 indicates that the Dedanites lived on the Arabian Peninsula.

Not Left Behind

Therefore, son of man, prophesy and say to Gog: "This is what the Sovereign LORD says: 'In that day, when my people Israel are living in safety, will you not take notice of it? You will come from your place in the far north, you and many nations with you, all of them riding on horses, a great horde, a mighty army. You will advance against my people Israel like a cloud that covers the land. In days to come, O Gog, I will bring you against my land, so that the nations may know me when I show myself holy through you before their eyes.'"

(Ezekiel 38:14-16)

This passage summarizes the previous verses. Gog and his allies will attack the people of Israel who believe they are living in safety with a large and powerful army. Then the Lord says "I will bring you against my land, so that the nations may know me when I show myself holy through you before their eyes." The Lord will be glorified!

This is what the Sovereign LORD says: "Are you not the one I spoke of in former days by my servants the prophets of Israel? At that time they prophesied for years that I would bring you against them. This is what will happen in that day: When Gog attacks the land of Israel, my hot anger will be aroused, declares the Sovereign LORD. In my zeal and fiery wrath I declare that at that time there shall be a great earthquake in the land of Israel. The fish of the sea, the birds of the air, the beasts of the field, every creature that moves along the ground, and all the people on the face of the earth will tremble at my presence. The mountains will be overturned, the cliffs will crumble and every wall will fall to the ground. I will summon a sword against Gog on all my mountains," declares the Sovereign LORD. "Every man's sword will be against his brother. I will execute judgment upon him with plague and bloodshed; I will pour down torrents of rain, hailstones and burning sulfur on him and on his troops and on the many nations with him. And so I will show my greatness and my holiness, and I will make myself known in the sight of many nations. Then they will know that I am the LORD."

(Ezekiel 38:17-23)

When the three hundred trumpets sounded, the LORD caused the men throughout the camp to turn on each other with their swords.

(Judges 7:22a)

This isn't the first time that a prophet of Israel has prophesied that Gog will attack Israel. Gog will not be defeated by Israel's military or even the military of the United States, but by the

Not Left Behind

Lord Himself. Every creature on land, sea, and air and *"all the people on the face of the earth"* will tremble at the Lord's presence. There will be "a great earthquake in the land of Israel." The attackers will turn on themselves, as in the story of Gideon in Judges 7 and a judgment of *"plague and bloodshed… torrents of rain, hailstones and burning sulfur"* on Gog *"and his troops and the many nations with him."*

> *Son of man, prophesy against Gog and say: "This is what the Sovereign LORD says: 'I am against you, O Gog, chief prince of Meshech and Tubal. I will turn you around and drag you along. I will bring you from the far north and send you against the mountains of Israel. Then I will strike your bow from your left hand and make your arrows drop from your right hand. On the mountains of Israel you will fall, you and all your troops and the nations with you. I will give you as food to all kinds of carrion birds and to the wild animals. You will fall in the open field, for I have spoken,' declares the Sovereign LORD. 'I will send fire on Magog and on those who live in safety in the coastlands, and they will know that I am the LORD.'"*
>
> (Ezekiel 39:1-6)

The Lord is telling *"Gog, the chief prince of*

Meshach and Tubal" that He is against him and that He is in control. They may think it is their idea to attack Israel, but in reality, the Sovereign Lord is going to *"drag them"* along from *"the far north"* to *"the mountains of Israel."* Then the Sovereign Lord will disarm them and give them "as food to all kinds of carrion birds and to the wild animals."

Not only will the Sovereign Lord destroy the attacking armies, but He *"will send fire on Magog and on those who live in safety in the coastlands."* Why would the Lord do this? So "they will know that I am the LORD."

Who are those who live in safety in the coastlands?" It can be almost any country or countries who think they are safe from attack. But as we saw on September 11, 2001, no country is safe from attack.

> *I will make known my holy name among my people Israel. I will no longer let my holy name be profaned, and the nations will know that I the LORD am the Holy One in Israel. It is coming! It will surely take place, declares the Sovereign LORD. This is the day I have spoken of.*
> (Ezekiel 39:7-8)

The Lord wants His name to be holy and known among His people Israel. The Lord does not want His holy name to be profaned. He

Not Left Behind

wants all the nations to "know that I the LORD am the Holy One in Israel."

"Then those who live in the towns of Israel will go out and use the weapons for fuel and burn them up—the small and large shields, the bows and arrows, the war clubs and spears. For seven years they will use them for fuel. They will not need to gather wood from the fields or cut it from the forests, because they will use the weapons for fuel. And they will plunder those who plundered them and loot those who looted them," declares the Sovereign LORD.

(Ezekiel 39:9-10)

After the Lord wipes out the invaders, the inhabitants of "the towns of Israel will go out and use the weapons for fuel and burn them up." There will be so many weapons left by the invades that it will take the people of Israel seven years to deplete the supply. That would be an awful of wood or possibly some nuclear weapons whose warheads can be converted to be used in a nuclear power plant.

On that day I will give Gog a burial place in Israel, in the valley of those who travel east toward the Sea. It will block the way of travelers, because

Glenn Tuley

Gog and all his hordes will be buried there. So it will be called the Valley of Hamon Gog.
(Ezekiel 39:11)

A special burial place will be created for all the bodies of the dead *"in the valley of those who travel east toward the Sea."* The burials will *"block the way of travelers"* probably due to the volume of bodies.

"For seven months the house of Israel will be burying them in order to cleanse the land. All the people of the land will bury them, and the day I am glorified will be a memorable day for them," declares the Sovereign LORD.
(Ezekiel 39:12-13)

Seven months of burials is a lot of burials. There will be so many that the entire country will participate in the burials. Of course, the day the Lord destroys the invading armies "will be a memorable day" to the people of Israel.

Men will be regularly employed to cleanse the land. Some will go throughout the land and, in addition to them, others will bury those that remain on the ground. At the end of the seven months they will begin their search. As they go through the land and one of them sees a human bone, he will set up a marker beside it until the gravediggers have

Not Left Behind

buried it in the Valley of Hamon Gog. (Also a town called Hamonah will be there.) And so they will cleanse the land.
(Ezekiel 39:14-16)

As part of the process of cleansing the land, men will be hired to search for remains that were not buried during the first seven months. They will mark the remains for the gravediggers who will bury them with the others.

Son of man, this is what the Sovereign LORD says: "Call out to every kind of bird and all the wild animals: 'Assemble and come together from all around to the sacrifice I am preparing for you, the great sacrifice on the mountains of Israel. There you will eat flesh and drink blood. You will eat the flesh of mighty men and drink the blood of the princes of the earth as if they were rams and lambs, goats and bulls—all of them fattened animals from Bashan. At the sacrifice I am preparing for you, you will eat fat till you are glutted and drink blood till you are drunk. At my table you will eat your fill of horses and riders, mighty men and soldiers of every kind,' declares the Sovereign LORD."
(Ezekiel 39:17-20)

This paragraph expands upon verse 4. *"Every*

Glenn Tuley

kind of bird and all the wild animals" will be invited to feast on a "sacrifice" of the bodies of the invaders of all ranks.

> *I will display my glory among the nations, and all the nations will see the punishment I inflict and the hand I lay upon them. From that day forward the house of Israel will know that I am the LORD their God. And the nations will know that the people of Israel went into exile for their sin, because they were unfaithful to me. So I hid my face from them and handed them over to their enemies, and they all fell by the sword. I dealt with them according to their uncleanness and their offenses, and I hid my face from them.*
> (Ezekiel 39:21-24)

The Lord will be glorified "among the nations, and all the nations will see the punishment I inflict and the hand I will lay upon them." There will be a return to the Lord, "From that day forward the house of Israel will know that I am the LORD their God." I find it significant that the Lord says that "the nations will know that the people of Israel went into exile for their sin" of being unfaithful to the Lord.

> *Therefore this is what the Sovereign LORD says: "I will now bring Jacob back from captivity and*

Not Left Behind

will have compassion on all the people of Israel, and I will be zealous for my holy name. They will forget their shame and all the unfaithfulness they showed toward me when they lived in safety in their land with no one to make them afraid. When I have brought them back from the nations and have gathered them from the countries of their enemies, I will show myself holy through them in the sight of many nations. Then they will know that I am the LORD their God, for though I sent them into exile among the nations, I will gather them to their own land, not leaving any behind. I will no longer hide my face from them, for I will pour out my Spirit on the house of Israel, declares the Sovereign LORD."

(Ezekiel 39:25-29)

The Sovereign LORD declares that He will bring the descendants of *"Jacob back from captivity and will have compassion on all the people of Israel, and I will be zealous for my holy name."* The Lord will show great enthusiasm for His reputation. *"Then they will know that I am the LORD their God"* and even though the Lord "sent them into exile among the nations," He *"will gather them to their own land, not leaving any behind."* This passage ends with a promise of the Lord. *"I will no longer hide my face from them, for I will pour out my Spirit on the house of Israel, declares the Sovereign LORD."*

Glenn Tuley

The big question regarding Chapters 38 and 39 of Ezekiel is "Do the events described are taking place before the Tribulation or at the end of it?" From the text itself in Ezekiel, it is inconclusive.

Chapter 13

DANIEL

Completed about 530 BC (portions written earlier).

Glenn Tuley

While I was speaking and praying, confessing my sin and the sin of my people Israel and making my request to the LORD my God for his holy hill- while I was still in prayer, Gabriel, the man I had seen in the earlier vision, came to me in swift flight about the time of the evening sacrifice. He instructed me and said to me, "Daniel, I have now come to give you insight and understanding."

(Daniel 9:20-22)

While Daniel was praying, the angel Gabriel, who had appeared to him in a previous vision, appeared and told Daniel that he have to give him *"insight and understanding."*

Seventy 'sevens' are decreed for your people and your holy city to finish transgression, to put an end to sin, to atone for wickedness, to bring in everlasting righteousness, to seal up vision and prophecy and to anoint the most holy.

Know and understand this: From the issuing of the decree to restore and rebuild Jerusalem until the Anointed One, the ruler, comes, there will be seven 'sevens,' and sixty-two 'sevens.' It will be rebuilt with streets and a trench, but in times of trouble. After the sixty-two 'sevens,' the Anointed One will be cut off and will have nothing. The people of the ruler who will come will destroy

Not Left Behind

the city and the sanctuary. The end will come like a flood: War will continue until the end, and desolations have been decreed. He will confirm a covenant with many for one 'seven.' In the middle of the 'seven' he will put an end to sacrifice and offering. And on a wing of the temple he will set up an abomination that causes desolation, until the end that is decreed is poured out on him.
(Daniel 9:24-27)

This is the *"70 Weeks"* of Daniel. From this passage we know that the 70 sevens have two parts: 7 sevens and 62 sevens. The decree recorded by Nehemiah to restore and rebuild Jerusalem was made on March 16, 445 BC. If you do the calculations of 7 sevens + 62 sevens adjusted for the 360 day Jewish calendar and you get the time of Jesus' Triumphal Entry into Jerusalem.

After the Anointed One is *"cut off,"* Jerusalem and the sanctuary will be destroyed again (as happened in 70 AD). Then there is the last seven. *"He will confirm a covenant with many for one 'seven.' In the middle of the 'seven' he will put and end to the sacrifice and offering."* We will see a covenant or treaty for seven years that will allow a resumption of sacrifice and offerings on the Temple Mount, but in the middle of the seven years some excuse will be found to abrogate the portion of the treaty relating to sacrifice and offerings.

Glenn Tuley

Now then, I tell you the truth: Three more kings will appear in Persia, and then a fourth, who will be far richer than all the others. When he has gained power by his wealth, he will stir up everyone against the kingdom of Greece. Then a mighty king will appear, who will rule with great power and do as he pleases. After he has appeared, his empire will be broken up and parceled out toward the four winds of heaven. It will not go to his descendants, nor will it have the power he exercised, because his empire will be uprooted and given to others.

(Daniel 11:2-4)

Daniel is recording a prophesy that describes the future empires that will rule over the land of Israel. This passage tells how Persia gets replaced by Greece as the leading power. The *"mighty king who will appear, who will rule with great power and do as he pleases"* is Alexander the Great. When he died his empire was *"broken up and parceled out toward the four winds of heaven"* and the parcels went to his generals not his descendants.

The king of the South will become strong, but one of his commanders will become even stronger than he and will rule his own kingdom with great power. After some years, they will become allies. The daughter of the king of the South will go to

Not Left Behind

the king of the North to make an alliance, but she will not retain her power, and he and his power will not last. In those days she will be handed over, together with her royal escort and her father and the one who supported her.
(Daniel 11:5-6)

The king of the South will send his daughter to the king of the North to make an alliance (these directions "South" and "North" are in relation to Israel). The diplomacy is not ultimately successful. Verses 7-28 describe various battles between the *"king of the North"* and the *"king of the South."*

At the appointed time he will invade the South again, but this time the outcome will be different from what it was before. Ships of the western coastlands will oppose him, and he will lose heart. Then he will turn back and vent his fury against the holy covenant. He will return and show favor to those who forsake the holy covenant.
(Daniel 11:29-30)

The king of the North will attack the king of the South again, but gets opposed by *"ships of the western coastlands."* The Hebrew word that is translated *"western coastlands"* is *"Kittim"* which originally referred to Cyprus, but grew to include the western Mediterranean coastlands. Kittim was a grandson of Noah whose descendants initially inhabited Cyprus and were believed to have migrated to the west on ships.

As a result of his defeat, "he will turn back and vent his fury against the holy covenant" and "show favor to those who forsake the holy covenant."

> *So when you see standing in the holy place 'the abomination that causes desolation,' spoken of through the prophet Daniel—let the reader understand—then let those who are in Judea flee to the mountains.*
> (Matthew 24:15-16)

> *His armed forces will rise up to desecrate the temple fortress and will abolish the daily sacrifice. Then they will set up the abomination that causes desolation. With flattery he will corrupt those who have violated the covenant, but the people who know their God will firmly resist him.*
> (Daniel 11:31-32)

The military of the North will *"desecrate the temple fortress"* simply by entering the temple area where Gentiles are not allowed and then they *"will abolish the daily sacrifice."* The abolishment of the daily sacrifice is mentioned again in Daniel 12.

After abolishing the daily sacrifice, *"they will set*

Not Left Behind

up the abomination that causes desolation." In the first fulfillment of this passage a statue of Zeus was set up in the Temple area. Jesus tells us in Matthew 24 that there will be a second fulfillment.

The king of the North will use flattery to *"corrupt those who have violated the covenant, but the people who know their God will firmly resist him."*

> *Those who are wise will instruct many, though for a time they will fall by the sword or be burned or captured or plundered. When they fall, they will receive a little help, and many who are not sincere will join them. Some of the wise will stumble, so that they may be refined, purified and made spotless until the time of the end, for it will still come at the appointed time.*
>
> (Daniel 11:33-35)

Who are *"those who are wise?"* Probably those who know the Lord and the Bible and live accordingly. The *"wise will instruct many"* and they will resist the king of the North and *"for a time they will fall by the sword or be burned or captured or plundered."* Those in the resistance will not get much help and many who join them will not have sincere motives.

"Some of the wise will stumble" in order *"that they may be refined, purified and made spotless until the time of the end, for it will still come at the appointed time."* That does not sound like the *"prosperity gospel,"* where

Glenn Tuley

'God wants everyone who follows him to get rich' to me.

> *The king will do as he pleases. He will exalt and magnify himself above every god and will say unheard-of things against the God of gods. He will be successful until the time of wrath is completed, for what has been determined must take place. He will show no regard for the gods of his fathers or for the one desired by women, nor will he regard any god, but will exalt himself above them all. Instead of them, he will honor a god of fortresses; a god unknown to his fathers he will honor with gold and silver, with precious stones and costly gifts. He will attack the mightiest fortresses with the help of a foreign god and will greatly honor those who acknowledge him. He will make them rulers over many people and will distribute the land at a price.*
>
> (Daniel 11:36-39)

This passage expresses the attitude of the king of the North. It also expresses the attitude of the Antichrist: *"do as he pleases, ...exalt and magnify himself above every god and will say unheard of things against the God of gods."* The good news is that even though he *"will be successful until the time of wrath is completed,"* his success will only be temporary.

At the time of the end the king of the South will

Not Left Behind

engage him in battle, and the king of the North will storm out against him with chariots and cavalry and a great fleet of ships. He will invade many countries and sweep through them like a flood. He will also invade the Beautiful Land. Many countries will fall, but Edom, Moab and the leaders of Ammon will be delivered from his hand. He will extend his power over many countries; Egypt will not escape. He will gain control of the treasures of gold and silver and all the riches of Egypt, with the Libyans and Nubians in submission. But reports from the east and the north will alarm him, and he will set out in a great rage to destroy and annihilate many. He will pitch his royal tents between the seas at the beautiful holy mountain. Yet he will come to his end, and no one will help him.

(Daniel 11:40-45)

The king of the South *"will engage him in battle"* and the king of the North will counter-attack, invading *"the Beautiful Land"* (Israel).

"Many countries will fall, but Edom, Moab and the leaders of Ammon will be delivered from his hand." The Edomites, Moabites and Ammonites lived in what is modern Jordan. Ammon is the modern capital of Jordan.

"He will extend his power over many countries; Egypt will not escape. He will gain control of the treasures

of gold and silver and all the riches of Egypt, with the Libyans and Nubians in submission." The king of the North will control Egypt, Libya, and the Sudan along with all their wealth.

But he will not like what he hears form the east and the north. He *"will set out in a rage to destroy and annihilate many."*

"He will pitch his royal tents" at the Temple Mount in Jerusalem. *"Yet he will come to his end, and no one will help him."*

> *At that time Michael, the great prince who protects your people, will arise. There will be a time of distress such as has not happened from the beginning of nations until then. But at that time your people—everyone whose name is found written in the book—will be delivered.*
>
> (Daniel 12:1)

The the Archangel Michael, who protects Israel will arise. *"There will be a time of distress such as has not happened from the beginning of nations until then."* Jesus used similar words in Mark 13 when commanding his disciples to pray "the *abomination that causes desolation… will not take place in winter."*

Then Daniel is told that *"at that time your people—everyone whose name is found written in the book-will be delivered."* Pre-tribulationists argue that this verse says that the Rapture or gathering of the elect

Not Left Behind

will take place at the beginning of the Tribulation or *"time of distress."* If that were true, then why would there be any need to mention the *"time of distress such as has not happened from the beginning of nations until then"* since *"everyone whose name is found written in the book"* would not see it?

> *Multitudes who sleep in the dust of the earth will awake: some to everlasting life, others to shame and everlasting contempt.*
> (Daniel 12:2)

This could be describing a single resurrection of the dead includes some who do not get *"everlasting life"* or it could be part of a high level description of the end times that summarizes details.

> *Those who are wise will shine like the brightness of the heavens, and those who lead many to righteousness, like the stars for ever and ever. But you, Daniel, close up and seal the words of the scroll until the time of the end. Many will go here and there to increase knowledge.*
> (Daniel 12:3-4)

Daniel is told to *"close up and seal the words of the scroll until the time of the end."* People are not expected to fully understand the prophesy until the time of the end. The wise will recognize it.

> *Then I, Daniel, looked, and there before me stood two others, one on this bank of the river and one on the opposite bank. One of them said to the man clothed in linen, who was above the waters of the river, "How long will it be before these astonishing things are fulfilled?"*
> (Daniel 12:5-6)

Of course, Daniel wanted to know *"How long will it be before these astonishing things are fulfilled?"*

> *The man clothed in linen, who was above the waters of the river, lifted his right hand and his left hand toward heaven, and I heard him swear by him who lives forever, saying, "It will be for a time, times and half a time. When the power of the holy people has been finally broken, all these things will be completed."*
> (Daniel 12:7)

The NIV footnotes say that *"a time, times and a half a time"* could also be translated as *"a year, two years and half a year"* or three and a half years.

> *I heard, but I did not understand. So I asked, "My lord, what will the outcome of all this be?"*
> (Daniel 12:8)

Not Left Behind

Daniel didn't comprehend the meaning of what he heard so he asked *"what will the outcome of this be?"*

> *He replied, "Go your way, Daniel, because the words are closed up and sealed until the time of the end. Many will be purified, made spotless and refined, but the wicked will continue to be wicked. None of the wicked will understand, but those who are wise will understand."*
> (Daniel 12:9-10)

Daniel is told to go about his business, *"because the words are closed up and sealed until the time of the end."* Believers *"will be purified, made spotless and refined,"* while those who refuse to trust in the Lord will continue in their ways. *"None of the wicked will understand, but those who are wise will understand."*

> *From the time that the daily sacrifice is abolished and the abomination that causes desolation is set up, there will be 1,290 days. Blessed is the one who waits for and reaches the end of the 1,335 days.*
> (Daniel 12:11-12)

It will be about 3½ years (1,290 days) from the time *"the daily sacrifice is abolished and the abomination that causes desolation is set up."* "Blessed is the one

Glenn Tuley

who waits for and reaches the end of the 1,335 days" (3½ years plus 45 days).

Chapter 14

JOEL

Written around 900 BC.

Glenn Tuley

And afterward, I will pour out my Spirit on all people. Your sons and daughters will prophesy, your old men will dream dreams, your young men will see visions. Even on my servants, both men and women, I will pour out my Spirit in those days.

(Joel 2:28-29)

In the end times the Holy Spirit will be active. Young men and women *"will prophesy."* *"Old men will dream dreams"* and *"young men will see visions."* The Lord will pour out his Spirit on *"both men and women."* in the last days.

I will show wonders in the heavens and on the earth, blood and fire and billows of smoke. The sun will be turned to darkness and the moon to blood before the coming of the great and dreadful day of the LORD.

(Joel 2:30-31)

The Lord *"will show wonders in the heavens." "On earth"* there will be *"blood and fire and billows of smoke."* This sounds like either war or meteors to me.

And everyone who calls on the name of the LORD will be saved; for on Mount Zion and in Jerusalem there will be deliverance, as the LORD has said, among the survivors whom the LORD calls.

(Joel 2:32)

Not Left Behind

On the first Day of Pentecost after Jesus' Resurrection, Peter quoted Joel 2:28-32, up to *"And everyone who calls on the name of the LORD will be saved."* While Peter was emphasizing pouring out of the Holy Spirit, there is more: *"for on Mount Zion and in Jerusalem there will be deliverance."*

> *In those days and at that time, when I restore the fortunes of Judah and Jerusalem...*
>
> (Joel 3:1)

Judah and Jerusalem will be restored economically.

> *I will gather all nations and bring them down to the Valley of Jehoshaphat. There I will enter into judgment against them concerning my inheritance, my people Israel, for they scattered my people among the nations and divided up my land. They cast lots for my people and traded boys for prostitutes; they sold girls for wine that they might drink.*
>
> (Joel 3:2-3)

The Lord will gather the nations to the Valley of Jehoshaphat to judge them concerning how they treated Israel.

Glenn Tuley

Now what have you against me, O Tyre and Sidon and all you regions of Philistia? Are you repaying me for something I have done? If you are paying me back, I will swiftly and speedily return on your own heads what you have done. For you took my silver and my gold and carried off my finest treasures to your temples. You sold the people of Judah and Jerusalem to the Greeks, that you might send them far from their homeland.
(Joel 3:4-6)

Tyre and Sidon are cities in what is now Lebanon. Philistia is land of the Philistines who lived in the area that is basically Gaza. This paragraph gives specific charges against Tyre, Sidon, and the regions of Philistia.

"See, I am going to rouse them out of the places to which you sold them, and I will return on your own heads what you have done. I will sell your sons and daughters to the people of Judah, and they will sell them to the Sabeans, a nation far away." The LORD has spoken.
(Joel 3:7-8)

The Lord is going to *"rouse them out of the places to which you have sold them."* This implies that *"the people of Judah and Jerusalem"* who where sold to the Greeks were asleep or not fully alert. The

Not Left Behind

Sabeans were we located in what is now southern Saudi Arabia and Yemen.

He will judge between the nations and will settle disputes for many peoples. They will beat their swords into plowshares and their spears into pruning hooks. Nation will not take up sword against nation, nor will they train for war anymore.

(Isaiah 2:4)

Proclaim this among the nations: Prepare for war! Rouse the warriors! Let all the fighting men draw near and attack Beat your plowshares into swords and your pruning hooks into spears. Let the weakling say, "I am strong!" Come quickly, all you nations from every side, and assemble there. Bring down your warriors, O LORD!

(Joel 3:9-11)

The Lord is calling the nations to war so He can punish them. This is in stark contrast to Isaiah 2:4 and Micah 4:3 where weapons of war are turned into farm implements. Micah 4:3 is identical except "the nations" is replaced with *"many peoples."*

The first part of this passage repeats verse 3. *"Jehoshaphat"* means *"the Lord judges."* The *"valley of decision"* is the place where the Lord judges.

Glenn Tuley

Let the nations be roused; let them advance into the Valley of Jehoshaphat, for there I will sit to judge all the nations on every side. Swing the sickle, for the harvest is ripe. Come, trample the grapes, for the winepress is full and the vats overflow—so great is their wickedness! Multitudes, multitudes in the valley of decision! For the day of the LORD is near in the valley of decision.

The sun and moon will be darkened, and the stars no longer shine. The LORD will roar from Zion and thunder from Jerusalem; the earth and the sky will tremble. But the LORD will be a refuge for his people, a stronghold for the people of Israel.
(Joel 3:12-16)

"The sun and the moon will be darkened, and stars will no longer shine." Sounds a lot like Matthew 24:29, which is placed just before Jesus' return. Based on this we can be confident in saying that this is describing events of the end times.

Chapter 15

ZECHARIAH

Written around 480 BC.

Glenn Tuley

Rejoice greatly, O Daughter of Zion! Shout, Daughter of Jerusalem! See, your king comes to you, righteous and having salvation, gentle and riding on a donkey, on a colt, the foal of a donkey.
(Zechariah 9:9)

On the original Palm Sunday Jesus entered Jerusalem riding on a donkey's colt to the praise of the daughters of Jerusalem.

This took place to fulfill what was spoken through the prophet: "Say to the Daughter of Zion, 'See, your king comes to you, gentle and riding on a donkey, on a colt, the foal of a donkey.'"
(Matthew 21:4-5)

I will take away the chariots from Ephraim and the war-horses from Jerusalem, and the battle bow will be broken. He will proclaim peace to the nations. His rule will extend from sea to sea and from the River to the ends of the earth.
(Zechariah 9:10)

The Lord *"will take away the chariots from Ephraim and the war horses from Jerusalem, and the battle bow will be broken."* Ephraim was the tribe that hosted the government of the Northern Kingdom, when Israel split after the death of Solomon. Ephraim also occupied a significant portion of what is

Not Left Behind

now known as *"the West Bank."* It doesn't matter how you interpret this because, *"He will proclaim peace to the nations. His rule will extend from sea to sea and from the River to the ends of the earth."* Everything will be under His dominion!

Then the LORD will appear over them; his arrow will flash like lightning. The Sovereign LORD will sound the trumpet; he will march in the storms of the south, and the LORD Almighty will shield them. They will destroy and overcome with slingstones. They will drink and roar as with wine; they will be full like a bowl used for sprinkling the corners of the altar.

(Zechariah 9:14-15)

The LORD will appear with a *"flash like lightning"* and the *"sound of the trumpet"* and *"will march in the storms of the south."* The *"LORD Almighty will shield"* His people and *"they will destroy and overcome with slingstones."* A slingstone is a relatively insignificant weapon, unless your name is Goliath!

A day of the LORD is coming when your plunder will be divided among you. I will gather all the nations to Jerusalem to fight against it; the city will be captured, the houses ransacked, and the women raped. Half of the city will go into exile, but the rest of the people will not be taken from the city.

(Zechariah 14:1-2)

Glenn Tuley

As in the prophesies in Joel, the Lord is gathering the nations to attack Israel. Zechariah records the Lord saying that Jerusalem will be attacked and *"the city will be captured, the houses ransacked, and the women raped."* Only half the people will be taken from the city into exile.

> *Then the LORD will go out and fight against those nations, as he fights in the day of battle. On that day his feet will stand on the Mount of Olives, east of Jerusalem, and the Mount of Olives will be split in two from east to west, forming a great valley, with half of the mountain moving north and half moving south. You will flee by my mountain valley, for it will extend to Azel. You will flee as you fled from the earthquake in the days of Uzziah king of Judah. Then the LORD my God will come, and all the holy ones with him.*
>
> (Zechariah 14:3-5)

The Lord will fight against the nations that attack Israel. He *"will stand on the Mount of Olives"* which *"will be split in two from east to west, forming a great valley." "Then the LORD my God will come, and all the holy ones with him."*

> *On that day there will be no light, no cold or frost. It will be a unique day, without daytime*

Not Left Behind

or nighttime—a day known to the LORD. When evening comes, there will be light.
(Zechariah 14:6-7)

That *"will be a unique day:" "no light, no cold or frost," "without daytime or nighttime." "When evening comes, there will be light"* probably because of the presence of the Lord.

On that day living water will flow out from Jerusalem, half to the eastern sea and half to the western sea, in summer and in winter.
(Zechariah 14:8)

A spring of *"living water"* will erupt in Jerusalem, probably in that area of the Temple Mount, and will flow in two directions to the Mediterranean and the Dead Sea.

The LORD will be king over the whole earth. On that day there will be one LORD, and his name the only name.
(Zechariah 14:9)

Jesus wins in the end. When He returns, he will be recognized as the one and only Lord.

The whole land, from Geba to Rimmon, south of Jerusalem, will become like the Arabah.

Glenn Tuley

But Jerusalem will be raised up and remain in its place, from the Benjamin Gate to the site of the First Gate, to the Corner Gate, and from the Tower of Hananel to the royal winepresses. It will be inhabited; never again will it be destroyed. Jerusalem will be secure.

(Zechariah 14:10-11)

Geba, now called El Geba, is about 6 miles north of Jerusalem and Rimmon is about 35 miles south of Jerusalem. The earthquake in verse 4 will create a plain *"like the Arabah." "Jerusalem will be secure,"* never to be destroyed again.

This is the plague with which the LORD will strike all the nations that fought against Jerusalem: Their flesh will rot while they are still standing on their feet, their eyes will rot in their sockets, and their tongues will rot in their mouths. On that day men will be stricken by the LORD with great panic. Each man will seize the hand of another, and they will attack each other. Judah too will fight at Jerusalem. The wealth of all the surrounding nations will be collected— great quantities of gold and silver and clothing.. A similar plague will strike the horses and mules, the camels and donkeys, and all the animals in those camps.

(Zechariah 14:12-15)

Not Left Behind

Fighting against Jerusalem does not seem like it will be a healthy thing to do. *"The wealth of the surrounding nations will be collected."* It used to be common for traveling armies to carry their riches with them, but I can't think of an army that has done it in recent centuries. Maybe those nations who attack Jerusalem will pay reparations (monetary damages for damages caused by war).

Then the survivors from all the nations that have attacked Jerusalem will go up year after year to worship the King, the LORD Almighty, and to celebrate the Feast of Tabernacles. If any of the peoples of the earth do not go up to Jerusalem to worship the King, the LORD Almighty, they will have no rain. If the Egyptian people do not go up and take part, they will have no rain. The LORD will bring on them the plague he inflicts on the nations that do not go up to celebrate the Feast of Tabernacles. This will be the punishment of Egypt and the punishment of all the nations that do not go up to celebrate the Feast of Tabernacles.
(Zechariah 14:16-19)

This is obviously describing the Millennial Reign of Christ. The only King worthy of being worshipped and called *"the LORD Almighty"* is Jesus when He returns. This passage tells us that celebrating the Feast of Tabernacles will be required of everyone.

Glenn Tuley

On that day HOLY TO THE LORD will be inscribed on the bells of the horses, and the cooking pots in the LORD's house will be like the sacred bowls in front of the altar. Every pot in Jerusalem and Judah will be holy to the LORD Almighty, and all who come to sacrifice will take some of the pots and cook in them. And on that day there will no longer be a Canaanite in the house of the LORD Almighty.

(Zechariah 14:20-21)

The phrase *"HOLY TO THE LORD"* will be written on *"the bells of the horses, and the cooking pots in the LORD's house will be like the sacred bowls in from of the altar."* It is interesting to note that *"Every pot in Jerusalem and Judah will be holy to the LORD Almighty"* and they will be used by pilgrims who come to sacrifice to the Lord.

The last verse doesn't tell us if *"Canaanite"* refers to biological Canaanites who would have presumably taken part in the war against Jerusalem and been killed or if it refers to spiritual Canaanites who do not believe in the Lord. I believe it could be either or both interpretations, since anyone who did not want to worship King Jesus, probably could not bear being anywhere near Him!

Chapter 16

MALACHI

Written around 430 BC.

Glenn Tuley

"Surely the day is coming; it will burn like a furnace. All the arrogant and every evildoer will be stubble, and that day that is coming will set them on fire," says the LORD Almighty. "Not a root or a branch will be left to them. But for you who revere my name, the sun of righteousness will rise with healing in its wings. And you will go out and leap like calves released from the stall. Then you will trample down the wicked; they will be ashes under the soles of your feet on the day when I do these things," says the LORD Almighty.

(Malachi 4:1-3)

Judgment is coming: *"the arrogant and every evildoer"* will get burned up, but for those *"who revere my name, the sun of righteousness will rise with healing in its wings. And you will go out and leap like calves released from the stall."*

Remember the law of my servant Moses, the decrees and laws I gave him at Horeb for all Israel. See, I will send you the prophet Elijah before that great and dreadful day of the LORD comes. He will turn the hearts of the fathers to their children, and the hearts of the children to their fathers; or else I will come and strike the land with a curse.

(Malachi 4:5-6)

Not Left Behind

The prophet Elijah will be sent back before the *"great and dreadful day of the LORD comes."*

Chapter 17

Amos

Written around 750 BC.

Glenn Tuley

Woe to you who long for the day of the LORD!
Why do you long for the day of the LORD ?
That day will be darkness, not light.
(Amos 5:18)

Amos warns against longing *"for the day of the LORD!"* There *"will be darkness not light."*

It will be as though a man fled from a lion only to meet a bear, as though he entered his house and rested his hand on the wall only to have a snake bite him.
(Amos 5:19)

A very picturesque way of saying it will not be a fun time.

Will not the day of the LORD be darkness, not light—pitch-dark, without a ray of brightness?
(Amos 5:20)

Amos repeats the reference to the *"day of the LORD"* being a time of darkness.

Chapter 18

ZEPHANIAH

Written around 630 BC.

Glenn Tuley

"I will sweep away everything from the face of the earth," declares the LORD.
(Zephaniah 1:2)

The LORD declares that He *"will sweep away everything from the face of the earth."*

"I will sweep away both men and animals; I will sweep away the birds of the air and the fish of the sea. The wicked will have only heaps of rubble when I cut off man from the face of the earth," declares the LORD.
(Zephaniah 1:3)

In addition to men, animals, birds, and fish *"will be swept away,"* by the LORD. *"The wicked will only have heaps of rubble"* when man is cut off *"from the face of the earth."*

The great day of the LORD is near—near and coming quickly. Listen! The cry on the day of the LORD will be bitter, the shouting of the warrior there. That day will be a day of wrath, a day of distress and anguish, a day of trouble and ruin, a day of darkness and gloom, a day of clouds and blackness, a day of trumpet and battle cry against the fortified cities and against the corner towers.
(Zephaniah 1:14-16)

Not Left Behind

There will be bitter crying on *"the day of the LORD."* It *"will be a day of wrath"* with *"distress and anguish"* and *"darkness and gloom"* and *"clouds and blackness."* The fortified cities will be hear the *"trumpet and battle cry."*

> *I will bring distress on the people and they will walk like blind men, because they have sinned against the LORD. Their blood will be poured out like dust and their entrails like filth. Neither their silver nor their gold will be able to save them on the day of the LORD's wrath. In the fire of his jealousy the whole world will be consumed, for he will make a sudden end of all who live in the earth.*
>
> (Zephaniah 1:17-18)

When the Lord returns to rule and reign, nothing will help you but your relationship with the Lord. He will not be impressed with your silver or gold or anything else you possess. If you are not *"ready to meet your maker,"* you will *"be in a world of hurt!"*

> *Gather together, gather together, O shameful nation, before the appointed time arrive and that day sweeps on like chaff, before the fierce anger of the LORD comes upon you, before the day of the LORD's wrath comes upon you. Seek the LORD, all you*

Glenn Tuley

humble of the land, you who do what he commands. Seek righteousness, seek humility; perhaps you will be sheltered on the day of the LORD's anger.
(Zephaniah 2:1-3)

Zephaniah is telling us that *"before the appointed time"* comes, Israel will be regathered. He warns that they need to do what the LORD commands, *"Seek righteousness, seek humility, perhaps you will be sheltered on the day of the LORD's anger."*

Chapter 19

REVELATION

Written around 100 AD.

Glenn Tuley

Look, he is coming with the clouds, and every eye will see him, even those who pierced him; and all peoples on earth will mourn because of him. So shall it be! Amen. "I am the Alpha and the Omega," says the Lord God, who is, and who was, and who is to come, the Almighty.

(Revelation 1:7-8)

When Jesus returns, everyone will see it, and some will not be happy about it. This quotes Daniel 7:13 and Zechariah 12:10.

Then I saw in the right hand of him who sat on the throne a scroll with writing on both sides and sealed with seven seals. And I saw a mighty angel proclaiming in a loud voice, "Who is worthy to break the seals and open the scroll?" But no one in heaven or on earth or under the earth could open the scroll or even look inside it. I wept and wept because no one was found who was worthy to open the scroll or look inside. Then one of the elders said to me, "Do not weep! See, the Lion of the tribe of Judah, the Root of David, has triumphed. He is able to open the scroll and its seven seals."

(Revelation 5:1-5)

John, while in a vision in heaven, sees a scroll with seven seals. Initially it is deemed that no one is worthy to break the seals. Then Jesus, *"the Lion*

Not Left Behind

of the tribe of Judah, the Root of David," is identified as being worthy.

> *I watched as the Lamb opened the first of the seven seals. Then I heard one of the four living creatures say in a voice like thunder, "Come!" I looked, and there before me was a white horse! Its rider held a bow, and he was given a crown, and he rode out as a conqueror bent on conquest.*
>
> (Revelation 6:1-2)

> *The next day John saw Jesus coming toward him and said, "Look, the Lamb of God, who takes away the sin of the world!"*
>
> (John 1:29)

When Jesus, "the Lamb of God," opened the first seal, John sees a rider on a white horse holding a bow. The rider is given a crown and he rides out "as a conqueror bent on conquest". The text does not identify the rider or who gave him a crown or who he intends to conquer.

> *When the Lamb opened the second seal, I heard the second living creature say, "Come!" Then another horse came out, a fiery red one. Its rider was given power to take peace from the earth and to make men slay each other. To him was given a large sword.*
>
> (Revelation 6:3-4)

Glenn Tuley

When Jesus opened the second seal, a fiery red horse came out. *"Its rider was given power to take peace from the earth and to make men slay each other."* The rider *"was given a large sword."*

> *When the Lamb opened the third seal, I heard the third living creature say, "Come!" I looked, and there before me was a black horse! Its rider was holding a pair of scales in his hand. Then I heard what sounded like a voice among the four living creatures, saying, "A quart of wheat for a day's wages, and three quarts of barley for a day's wages, and do not damage the oil and the wine!"*
> (Revelation 6:5-6)

Upon Jesus opening the third seal, a rider came forth on a black horse. This rider had a pair of scales in his hand. Then it was announced that a quart of wheat and three quarts of barley would cost a day's wages. A quart of wheat is about one day's worth of food. Barley is a cheaper grain for the poorer people.

The problem with a day's wages only buying a day's food is there is nothing left to feed his family or buy anything else. Of course that is not very good for the economy. The phrase "and do not damage the oil and wine" implies that the inflation in food prices are caused by crop damages.

Not Left Behind

When the Lamb opened the fourth seal, I heard the voice of the fourth living creature say, "Come!" I looked, and there before me was a pale horse! Its rider was named Death, and Hades was following close behind him. They were given power over a fourth of the earth to kill by sword, famine and plague, and by the wild beasts of the earth.
(Revelation 6:7-8)

When Jesus opened the fourth seal, John saw a rider on a pale horse. "Its rider was named Death, and Hades was following close behind him." Death and Hades "were given power over a fourth of the earth to kill by the sword, famine and plague, and by the wild beasts of the earth." It is not unusual for war to be followed by famine and plague. A shortage of food supply would likely cause wild beasts to attack humans.

What is really unusual about this passage is a quarter of the earth's population dying in a short period of time. That would be roughly 1.6 billion people dead out of an estimated 6.7 billion people (based on the world population at the end of 2007). There has not been such a decrease in the earth's population since the time of Noah.

When he opened the fifth seal, I saw under the altar the souls of those who had been slain

Glenn Tuley

because of the word of God and the testimony they had maintained. They called out in a loud voice, "How long, Sovereign Lord, holy and true, until you judge the inhabitants of the earth and avenge our blood?" Then each of them was given a white robe, and they were told to wait a little longer, until the number of their fellow servants and brothers who were to be killed as they had been was completed.

(Revelation 6:9-11)

The opening of the fifth seal made *"the souls of those who been slain because of the word of God and the testimony they maintained"* visible under the altar in heaven. *"They called out in a loud voice, 'How long, Sovereign Lord, holy and true, until you judge the inhabitants of the earth and avenge our blood?'"* They were given white robes and told *"to wait a little longer, until the number of their fellow servants and brothers who were to be killed as they had been was completed."* This passage foretells that the martyring of Christians will continue a little longer.

I watched as he opened the sixth seal. There was a great earthquake. The sun turned black like sackcloth made of goat hair, the whole moon turned blood red, and the stars in the sky fell to earth, as figs drop from a fig tree when shaken by a strong wind. The heavens receded like a scroll

Not Left Behind

being rolled up, and every mountain and island was removed from its place.
(Revelation 6:12-14)

The sixth seal releases a great earthquake. The side effects of the sun and moon changing colors could likely be the result of volcanic activity accompanying the earthquake. Gases being released and forming clouds could easily look like a scroll rolling up.. The 2011 earthquake off the coast of Japan that caused the devastating tsunami moved a GPS station 8 feet. That certainly qualifies as on instance of an *"island was removed from its place."* So, it is not too hard to imagine the horrifying effects of an event where "every mountain and island was removed from its place."

Stars falling from the sky could easily send everyone to man-made caves (fallout shelters).

Then the kings of the earth, the princes, the generals, the rich, the mighty, and everyone else, both slave and free, hid in caves and among the rocks of the mountains. They called to the mountains and the rocks, "Fall on us and hide us from the face of him who sits on the throne and from the wrath of the Lamb! For the great day of their wrath has come, and who can withstand it?"
(Revelation 6:15-17)

Glenn Tuley

Note that those who are asking the mountains and rocks to fall on them to hide them from the wrath of the probably do not have a relationship with Him. In one sense it is a silly request, since nothing can hide you from the Lamb of God!

And there was war in heaven. Michael and his angels fought against the dragon, and the dragon and his angels fought back. But he was not strong enough, and they lost their place in heaven. The great dragon was hurled down—that ancient serpent called the devil, or Satan, who leads the whole world astray. He was hurled to the earth, and his angels with him.

> *Then I heard a loud voice in heaven say: "Now have come the salvation and the power and the kingdom of our God, and the authority of his Christ. For the accuser of our brothers, who accuses them before our God day and night, has been hurled down. They overcame him by the blood of the Lamb and by the word of their testimony; they did not love their lives so much as to shrink from death. Therefore rejoice, you heavens and you who dwell in them! But woe to the earth and the sea, because the devil has gone down to you! He is filled with fury, because he knows that his time is short."*
>
> (Revelation 12:7-12)

Not Left Behind

After being kicked out of Heaven, the dragon (Satan or the Devil) was hurled down to earth. This is good news in Heaven, but it means trouble on Earth, because "he knows his time is short."

The beast was given a mouth to utter proud words and blasphemies and to exercise his authority for forty-two months.

(Revelation 13:5)

The beast will be free to say and do what he wants for three and a half years.

Chapter 20

HOW SHOULD WE LIVE?

What can and Should we do?

Glenn Tuley

Read the "Sermon on the Mount" (Matthew chapter 5 through 7) and remember its context. The Romans had conquered the land of the Jews and even renamed it "Palestine!" There were occupation armies in the country and tax monies were collected and sent to Rome.

> *"Blessed are those who are persecuted because of righteousness, for theirs is the kingdom of heaven. "Blessed are you when people insult you, persecute you and falsely say all kinds of evil against you because of me. Rejoice and be glad, because great is your reward in heaven, for in the same way they persecuted the prophets who were before you.*
> (Matthew 5:10-12)

The guidelines for living that Jesus gives in the "Sermon on the Mount" seem very appropriate for living through times of persecution, whether it is the Great Tribulation or not.

> *"You are the salt of the earth. But if the salt loses its saltiness, how can it be made salty again? It is no longer good for anything, except to be thrown out and trampled underfoot. "You are the light of the world. A town built on a hill cannot be hidden. Neither do people light a lamp and put it under a bowl. Instead they put it on its stand, and*

Not Left Behind

it gives light to everyone in the house. In the same way, let your light shine before others, that they may see your good deeds and glorify your Father in heaven.

(Matthew 5:13-16)

For this is the message you heard from the beginning: We should love one another.

(1 John 3:11)

We are to live lives that are noticeably different from the world around us.

Our behavior (the love that we show, not our "dos" and "don'ts") should set us apart so that those who know us will either know that we are Christians or will ask what makes us different, so that we will have the opportunity to tell us about Jesus in our lives and our relationship with Him.

"You have heard that it was said, 'Love your neighbor and hate your enemy.' But I tell you, love your enemies and pray for those who persecute you, that you may be children of your Father in heaven. He causes his sun to rise on the evil and the good, and sends rain on the righteous and the unrighteous. If you love those who love you, what reward will you get? Are not even the tax collectors doing that? And if you greet only your own people, what are you doing more than others?

Glenn Tuley

Do not even pagans do that? Be perfect, therefore, as your heavenly Father is perfect."

(Matthew 5:43-48)

Loving your enemies becomes easier once you start praying for them. Once you start praying for them, you start to see them as God sees them: people (like you) in need of a Savior!

And when you pray, do not be like the hypocrites, for they love to pray standing in the synagogues and on the street corners to be seen by others. Truly I tell you, they have received their reward in full. But when you pray, go into your room, close the door and pray to your Father, who is unseen. Then your Father, who sees what is done in secret, will reward you. And when you pray, do not keep on babbling like pagans, for they think they will be heard because of their many words. Do not be like them, for your Father knows what you need before you ask him.

(Matthew 6:5-8)

Praying for your enemies will bring you closer to the Lord and enhance your relationship with Him.

Do not judge, or you too will be judged. For in the same way you judge others, you will be judged, and

Not Left Behind

with the measure you use, it will be measured to you.
(Matthew 7:1-2)

If you want grace, give grace.
If someone needs correction, do it in private, like you would want someone to correct you.

This is how you can recognize the Spirit of God: Every spirit that acknowledges that Jesus Christ has come in the flesh is from God, but every spirit that does not acknowledge Jesus is not from God. This is the spirit of the antichrist, which you have heard is coming and even now is already in the world.
(1 John 4:2-3)

Watch out for false prophets. They come to you in sheep's clothing, but inwardly they are ferocious wolves. By their fruit you will recognize them. Do people pick grapes from thornbushes, or figs from thistles? Likewise, every good tree bears good fruit, but a bad tree bears bad fruit. A good tree cannot bear bad fruit, and a bad tree cannot bear good fruit. Every tree that does not bear good fruit is cut down and thrown into the fire. Thus, by their fruit you will recognize them.
(Matthew 7:15-20)

Glenn Tuley

Be on guard for people who preach the Gospel with a twist to it. Rarely, will a false prophet start with preaching outright lies. They usually start with subtle questioning of the truth or subtle deviations from the truth.

Know the Word. If you don't know the Word, you will have a hard time identifying and responding to false teaching. Most heresies are the truth with a subtle or not so subtle twist perverting the truth into a lie.

> *"Not everyone who says to me, 'Lord, Lord,' will enter the kingdom of heaven, but only the one who does the will of my Father who is in heaven. Many will say to me on that day, 'Lord, Lord, did we not prophesy in your name and in your name drive out demons and in your name perform many miracles?' Then I will tell them plainly, 'I never knew you. Away from me, you evildoers!'*
>
> (Matthew 7:21-23)

"Believers" who do not have personal relationship with the Lord are similar to false prophets, in their final judgment.

> *Dear friends, do not believe every spirit, but test the spirits to see whether they are from God, because many false prophets have gone out into the world.*
>
> (1 John 4:1)

Not Left Behind

How is your relationship with your Lord?

As God's co-workers we urge you not to receive God's grace in vain. For he says, "In the time of my favor I heard you, and in the day of salvation I helped you." I tell you, now is the time of God's favor, now is the day of salvation.

(2 Corinthians 6:1-2)

If your relationship with the Lord is not right now, now is the time to make it right.

Let everyone be subject to the governing authorities, for there is no authority except that which God has established. The authorities that exist have been established by God. Consequently, whoever rebels against the authority is rebelling against what God has instituted, and those who do so will bring judgment on themselves. For rulers hold no terror for those who do right, but for those who do wrong. Do you want to be free from fear of the one in authority? Then do what is right and you will be commended. For the one in authority is God's servant for your good. But if you do wrong, be afraid, for rulers do not bear the sword for no reason. They are God's servants, agents of wrath to bring punishment on the wrongdoer. Therefore, it is necessary to submit to the authorities, not only because of possible punishment but also as a matter of conscience.

(Romans 13:1-5)

Glenn Tuley

Follow the laws as much as you can in good conscience.

> *This is also why you pay taxes, for the authorities are God's servants, who give their full time to governing. Give to everyone what you owe them: If you owe taxes, pay taxes; if revenue, then revenue; if respect, then respect; if honor, then honor.*
> (Romans 13:6-7)

> *Submit yourselves for the Lord's sake to every human authority: whether to the emperor, as the supreme authority, or to governors, who are sent by him to punish those who do wrong and to commend those who do right. For it is God's will that by doing good you should silence the ignorant talk of foolish people. Live as free people, but do not use your freedom as a cover-up for evil; live as God's slaves. Show proper respect to everyone, love the family of believers, fear God, honor the emperor.*
> (1 Peter 2:13-17)

Don't do anything that would make you an unnecessary martyr. You can't stop the Antichrist. That is Jesus' job. So, unless He tells you to attack the Antichrist, doing so on your own is trying to put yourself in His place and setting yourself up for failure.

Not Left Behind

Since, according to Scripture, Jesus is the one who destroys the Antichrist, any attempt on your part will necessarily fail and make him seem justified in going after Christians.

Who is going to harm you if you are eager to do good? But even if you should suffer for what is right, you are blessed. "Do not fear their threats; do not be frightened." But in your hearts revere Christ as Lord. Always be prepared to give an answer to everyone who asks you to give the reason for the hope that you have. But do this with gentleness and respect, keeping a clear conscience, so that those who speak maliciously against your good behavior in Christ may be ashamed of their slander. For it is better, if it is God's will, to suffer for doing good than for doing evil.

(1 Peter 3:13-17)

The end of all things is near. Therefore be alert and of sober mind so that you may pray. Above all, love each other deeply, because love covers over a multitude of sins. Offer hospitality to one another without grumbling. Each of you should use whatever gift you have received to serve others, as faithful stewards of God's grace in its various forms. If anyone speaks, they should do so as one who speaks the very words of God. If anyone serves, they should do so with the strength God

Glenn Tuley

provides, so that in all things God may be praised through Jesus Christ. To him be the glory and the power for ever and ever. Amen.

(1 Peter 4:7-11)

About the Author

Glenn Tuley has a M.S. in Computer Science, with a Minor in History, from the University North Texas, where he was an AFROTC Distinguished Graduate, and a B.A. in History from The King's College, where "everyone had a Minor in Bible." He has read the Bible through in the KJV, NASB, NIV (1984), and Reina-Valera 1960.

Glenn retired from the Air Force, where he developed upgrades on AWACS aircraft and the World Wide Military Command and Control System, and tested software systems (B-1B and Joint STARS). He is also retired from the Brevard Public Schools as a Transportation Systems Technology Analyst.

Glenn's favorite job was being the Missionary Project Manager for HeartSprings International Ministries where he got to go on several missions trips to Huehuetenango, Guatemala. He also volunteered with Wycliffe Associates (the volunteer arm of Wycliffe Bible Translators).

Currently, Glenn volunteers with his local church, where he attends with his wife of 40 years, the youngest of his two daughters, her husband, and 4 grandchildren.

glenn@tuley.us

http://book.tuley.us

Made in the USA
Monee, IL
02 November 2021